"There are many unforgettable moments in Martin J. Smith's beautifully written, wry collection of essays about quirky strivers in the modern American Southwest. I'll never again look at the upturned tips of airplane wings without thinking of aviation pioneer Burt Rutan toiling away in the Mojave Desert. I'll never watch *Pulp Fiction* without thinking about the tumultuous life of surf guitarist Dick Dale, who lost his Newport Beach dream house but never gave up. And I will never think of a book tour without picturing the cross-country, do-it-yourself promotional trek that Smith took with a writer buddy and their four young children in rented minivans. When his son asks, 'Are we there yet?,' Smith takes it as an existential question. 'No,' he writes, 'I'm not there yet.' I beg to differ."

—ROBIN ABCARIAN, COLUMNIST, *LOS ANGELES TIMES*

MR. LAS VEGAS HAS A BAD KNEE

and Other Tales of the People, Places,
and Peculiarities of the Modern American Southwest

MARTIN J. SMITH

TWODOT®

GUILFORD, CONNECTICUT

A · TWODOT® · BOOK

An imprint of Globe Pequot
An imprint and registered trademark of Rowman & Littlefield

Distributed by NATIONAL BOOK NETWORK

British Library Cataloguing in Publication Information available

Library of Congress Cataloging-in-Publication Data

Name: Smith, Martin J., 1956- author.
Title: Mr. Las Vegas has a bad knee : and other tales of the people, places, and peculiarities of the modern American Southwest / Martin J. Smith.
Other titles: Tales of the people, places, and peculiarities of the modern American Southwest
Description: Guilford, Connecticut : TwoDot, [2017]
Identifiers: LCCN 2016052634 (print) | LCCN 2016052832 (ebook) | ISBN 9781493028443 (pbk.) | ISBN 9781493028450 (e-book)
Subjects: LCSH: Southwest, New—Biography—Anecdotes. | Southwest, New—Social life and customs—Anecdotes. | Celebrities—United States—Anecdotes.
Classification: LCC F785.5 .S55 2017 (print) | LCC F785.5 (ebook) | DDC 979—dc23
LC record available at https://lccn.loc.gov/2016052634

∞™ The paper used in this publication meets the minimum requirements of American National Standard for Information Sciences—Permanence of Paper for Printed Library Materials, ANSI/NISO Z39.48-1992.

Printed in the United States of America

For R. Thomas Berner, H. Eugene Goodwin, Patrick J. Kiger,
and all of the other journalistic mentors who taught me along the way

Contents

Foreword by David L. Ulin ix
Introduction: The Land of Id xi

CHAPTER 1: Mr. Las Vegas Has a Bad Knee 1
CHAPTER 2: Extinction Along Interstate 10. 9
CHAPTER 3: Looking for Big George Coyle. 15
CHAPTER 4: The Fall and Rise of a Guitar Hero 21
CHAPTER 5: Lesbian Cairn Terrier Owners, Unite! 33
CHAPTER 6: Are We There Yet? 39
CHAPTER 7: The Cinematic Landmark of *Red Asphalt* 49
CHAPTER 8: Lynne Cox's Incomparable Wake 55
CHAPTER 9: Lamenting Liberace 61
CHAPTER 10: The Birdman of Mojave. 65
CHAPTER 11: Honeymooning at Warp Speed. 75
CHAPTER 12: The Wild Duck Chase 83
CHAPTER 13: Woofers on Wheels. 95
CHAPTER 14: Buzz Aldrin's Traveling Tube of Glue 103
CHAPTER 15: The Mark of Mickey 111
CHAPTER 16: The Downside of Perfection 115
CHAPTER 17: Taking Tinseltown with "The Greatest" 123
CHAPTER 18: Life Begins at 150 135
CHAPTER 19: The Toilet-Valve Titan 143
CHAPTER 20: Corky Ra's Peculiar Master Plan 149
CHAPTER 21: Toenail Polish for Fluffy 159
CHAPTER 22: The Life and Death of AC-3 165

Contents

CHAPTER 23: SeaWorld's Six-Thousand-Pound PR Problem 179
CHAPTER 24: Aren't We All Just Squatters, Really? 187

Acknowledgments 191
About the Author 193

Foreword

By David L. Ulin

MARTIN J. SMITH IS ONTO SOMETHING. IT'S A SNEAKY KIND OF SOME-thing, the kind of something journalists notice when they've been on a beat, working a territory: a collision of ideas, of sensibilities, into a larger point of view. "Here's the thing about Southern California: Permanence is illusion. Legends wither. The past impedes the future," Smith writes in "Extinction Along Interstate 10," the story of the roadside dinosaurs of Cabazon. And yet, there's this as well, from his well-wrought portrait of surf guitar god Dick Dale: "[T]he best stories develop over time, stories in which character is revealed rather than exposed." Somewhere in between these two perspectives—the short and the long view, the sense that nothing matters and that everything does—the twenty-four essays in this collection unfold. "The Land of Id," Smith calls it in his introduction, and it's a label that applies.

The American Southwest, which is the landscape that Smith travels in these writings, is as it has ever been: a template, raw fodder for our nightmares and our dreams. If that sounds like hyperbole, so be it; the evidence, I want to tell you, bears it out. Consider the old timer's club he discovers in "Mr. Las Vegas Has a Bad Knee," his complex and moving portrait of Wayne Newton, which holds its final meeting "at the Stardust before it was imploded," before giving up entirely on the city's history. Could there be a more effective metaphor for the boom-and-bust mentality of the place, which is, after all, just a desert town that got very, very big?

These are the questions Smith raises, with his excursions, real and virtual. On a website called Meetup, he finds the three members of the lesbian cairn terrier owners of Orange County, which leads to a riff on subcultures and what they may or may not mean. The deathwatch outside Liberace's Palm Springs home encourages a meditation on the peculiar social glue of fame, not for the performer as much as for the fans. Elsewhere, Smith introduces a designer of experimental aircraft, a podiatrist who hit 2,750 free throws without a miss, and a toilet innovator about to be inducted into the Plumbing Hall of Fame. Dreamers, in other words, every one of them, of what Joan Didion once referred to as the golden dream.

Why is this important? Because it's disappearing, for one thing, as the culture homogenizes. But even more because it remains representative just the same. If Smith's book is about anything, it is about place, the way it gets inside us. And the Southwest . . . there is something about the space, the unformed landscape, that both terrifies and inspires, allowing us to see our limits and our possibilities. Thus, if on the one hand, Smith is tracking a lost world—"Lawyers have a philosophy in this country that people shouldn't be allowed to take risks," insists *Voyager* aircraft designer Burt Rutan. "You watch that. If someone tells you they have a proposition for you without any risks, watch out that he's not trying to take away your freedom"—it is a lost world that also is brave and new. Sound like a contradiction? That's the whole idea behind Smith's work in this collection, which traces (as it must) the middle ground between opposing, but not irreconcilable, perspectives: "Permanence is illusion" and "The best stories develop over time."

David L. Ulin is the author, most recently, of the novel *Ear to the Ground*, written with Paul Kolsby. A 2015 Guggenheim Fellow, his other books include *Sidewalking: Coming to Terms with Los Angeles*, a finalist for the PEN/Diamonstein-Spielvogel Award for the Art of the Essay, and *Writing Los Angeles: A Literary Anthology*, which won a California Book Award.

Introduction

The Land of Id

IN 1985, THE SAME YEAR I MOVED FROM THE EAST TO THE WEST, A seemingly upstanding Newport Beach, California, businessman named John Davis Sr. announced quite publicly that he wanted to buy a whorehouse.

Davis had put a *lot* of thought into this midlife career move. This was not some bling-encrusted pimp deciding to set up shop in a downtown tenement instead of having his girls work the bus station. This was a man who'd bought an obscure, year-old Salt Lake City corporation called Strong Point Inc. intending to use it as a legal shell for various businesses—and never mind that the company had no real assets or money, or that Davis and his primary partner already had a somewhat uneven history as businessmen. As Davis began looking for investment opportunities, he noticed a classified ad in the *Wall Street Journal* seeking buyers for a small Nevada town that included a brothel.

"I saw the representations of the earnings," he later told the *Los Angeles Times*, "[and] I thought, 'This looks very interesting.'"

Although that particular deal never panned out, Davis already was working on his Big Idea. He and his partner began touring Nevada brothels, their lustful eyes fixed not on the shapely working girls who greeted them as they arrived but instead on the bottom line of the brothel business. Eventually, Davis announced his plan to buy, for eighteen million dollars, one of the most famous legal brothels in the United States, the fabled Mustang Ranch in Storey County, Nevada, just outside Reno.

And where did he plan to get eighteen million dollars? That was where the story took a distinctive turn, one that, in my mind, marks it as a pure and unmistakable product of the modern American Southwest. His Big Idea—the stuff of which business-school legends are made—was his stated intention to operate the whorehouse as a public corporation, to become the first such enterprise in the United States to sell shares of the business to stockholders, to put control of the bordello in the hands of a board of directors whose job it would be to maximize shareholder value. Davis told me he hoped to use the Mustang Ranch as the keystone of his plan to operate a chain of whorehouses traversing the Interstate 80 corridor across the northern part of Nevada like a chain of Denny's road-food restaurants, except with an entirely different sort of grand-slam menu.

I chronicled Davis's ultimately doomed effort to create the country's first publicly held brothel during my first two years as a journalist based in Southern California. But looking back more than three decades later, I remember my first August 1985 encounter with Davis's Big Idea as the precise moment when I knew for sure that I was witnessing a much bigger reality: the ongoing story of an oft-idealized and misunderstood landscape that's like no other in the United States, and perhaps the world.

People in the American Southwest just *see* things differently than other people. Where others see accepted reality, Westerners see potential, opportunities, *possibility*. It's no accident that the "I think I can" mantras of personal-fulfillment huckster Anthony Robbins and the Crystal Cathedral's possibility-thinking Rev. Robert Schuller emanated from Southern California. Those guys understood what can happen when a critical mass of like-minded people get together. Like Robbins and Schuller, their followers were drawn to this self-motivated and instinctual Land of Id because here, unbound by convention, they know they can pursue their dreams and schemes without regard to reality as everyone else has defined it.

The Southwest is now—still—a place where a startling number of people approach life with the same appetite for risk and reward as poker champions and extreme athletes. They arrive as questing migrants, or spring fully formed from the landscape, with the same refreshingly cockeyed approach to life as John Davis Sr. You hear a lot about the Southwest, Southern California in particular, being a place where people come to reinvent themselves. I suppose that's true. But that reputation obscures the more important reality that a lot of pure invention goes on here as well.

Someone once described the region as a place created when a great force picked up the United States by the East Coast and shook it. Everything that was unattached, unstable, or willing to risk letting go found its way here. Does the region have more than its share of marginally delusional dreamers? Of course. Charles Manson was one of them, but then, so was Howard Hughes. So were William Shockley, who invented the transistor and paved the road to Silicon Valley, and gawky kid-wonks named Steve Jobs and Mark Zuckerberg. Just as it took someone with a peculiarly Western mindset to see the world's oldest profession in an entirely different way, it took an iconoclast such as Mojave-based aircraft designer Burt Rutan to question long-standing assumptions and see—reimagine—what flight could be. It took Orange County, California, marathon swimmer Lynne Cox to even imagine swimming without a wetsuit in the slushy waters of Antarctica, and then train herself to actually do it. It took a retired seventy-something podiatrist from Long Beach, Tom Amberry, to see the art of basketball free throw shooting as a purely mechanical process, to perfect it, and demonstrate his ability to the world by shooting for twelve straight hours—2,750 baskets in a row—without missing once. (Amberry only stopped because the health club where he set the Guinness world record needed its court back.) Who but a self-styled So Cal mystic would see and pursue good-old Egyptian-style mummification as a viable business opportunity during the go-go 1980s?

I was born in Alabama, raised in Pennsylvania, and have traveled everywhere from Europe to the Arctic Circle to northern Africa to Siberia to the Philippines, and my sense is that there are very real reasons why the American Southwest boasts more than its share of Nobel Prize laureates and inventors and entrepreneurs and artists, more than its share of premier athletes and con men and the kind of folk who prefer to live in a place where so many people assume limitless possibility, and where the past matters less than the future. Their infectious approach to life is palpable, like a smell or a taste or the phantom-tickle of something that brushes against your skin. You may not know exactly what it is, but you know it's there, as real and powerful as the mysterious force of celebrity.

I consider it a privilege to have chronicled many stories that, gathered together, actually help tell the much grander story of this special place at the turn of the millennium. From those tales emerges a snapshot of a place awash in eccentric dreamers and robust weirdness.

But the real value of this story collection, I believe, is that with each tale comes a postscript. Most writers get only one chance to tell the stories they discover. This book is my second chance. Sometimes, particularly in journalism, a writer has to tell a story before it has an ending, or before he or she has a chance to fully understand its broader themes. This collection of original nonfiction is my opportunity to revisit some of the heroes, iconoclasts, and cultural spasms I've documented during more than three decades as a journalist, but with the perspective that only time and distance can offer. They all fit together, improbably, into a hyperkinetic montage of a remarkable and endless frontier vastly different from the rest of the nation, a pulsing, tragicomic land of infinite possibilities.

If you're looking for a poster boy for it all, John Davis Sr.—with his potent combination of audacity, imagination, intelligence, humor, and perhaps a wee bit of mischief—works just as well as any. But looking back, I can finish his story. I now know, for example, what became of his Big Idea. It made national headlines for a while, briefly inflated the price of Strong Point's over-the-counter stock, even triggered an investigation by the federal Securities and Exchange Commission. In the end, though, it collapsed into a rubble-heap of lawsuits and died as a charred, smoking public failure.

But in the context of the bigger story about the place where that Big Idea was spawned, its failure is actually beside the point.

—Martin J. Smith, Granby, Colorado

CHAPTER ONE

Mr. Las Vegas Has a Bad Knee

The official Wayne Newton Tour, during which we learn the truth about the "historic" desert oasis, and the host is a no-show (2006)

WAYNE NEWTON ARRIVED IN LAS VEGAS AS A FRESH-FACED SEVENTEEN-year-old singing sensation, looking like the result of a science experiment involving Brylcreem and estrogen. It was 1959, and to put his Las Vegas tenure into perspective, that was the year Buddy Holly, Ritchie Valens, and the Big Bopper died, that Fidel Castro first took command of Cuba, and American Airlines scheduled its first transcontinental jet flight from Los Angeles to New York.

This is no way intended to make Wayne Newton feel old, since his pompadoured hair is every bit as black as the late Ronald Reagan's, but the guy has been a Las Vegas fixture for a very long time. And he's still there, overseeing his fifty-two-acre Casa de Shenandoah ranch, wowing the Wayniacs who flock to see him six nights a week, most recently at the Flamingo, and playing the role of the city's benevolent elder states-man. As proclaimed in the welcome banner at www.waynenewton.com (where the Wayne Wear Mug goes for just four dollars), Newton is "Mr. Las Vegas."

So, naturally, when Newton's people offered me a tour of Las Vegas guided by the ultimate Vegas insider, I couldn't say no. Who else would have such a sweeping grasp of local lore and history? Who better to narrate the tectonic shift that transformed the desert oasis into one of the fastest growing cities in America?

Wayne Newton in 2015 with his car collection at Casa de Shenandoah. This photograph by Christopher Devargas appeared in the Sept. 21, 2015, issue of the *Las Vegas Sun* to illustrate a story about Newton opening his longtime Las Vegas ranch, Casa de Shenandoah, as a museum.

I secretly was hoping for a glimpse at the behind-the-scenes workings of Sin City, where visitors are encouraged to unleash the beast within and the primary role of the immigrant class along the Strip seems to be handing out promotional cards for escort services. Newton's was a name that could open doors, and I knew the story might offer a rare glimpse at the copious consumption habits of Mr. Las Vegas himself. While he gives generously of his time and money to the USO and many other charitable causes, research also suggests that, despite some niggling bankruptcy problems in the early 1990s and a 2005 skirmish with the IRS, Newton's is a fast-lane life lived on private jets and Arabian horses, on personal yachts and helicopters, and behind the wheel of his fabulous cars. His star may have dimmed and his voice faltered in recent years, but he apparently has maintained his lifestyle by leveraging his fabled stage act into parallel careers in film and television.

In short, Wayne Newton seemed like a decent guy, a fascinating character, and the perfect escort into the neon-lit core of America's naked id. There was just one problem: actually connecting with Mr. Las Vegas.

Even though his own public relations agency had pitched the Wayne's World tour idea, it took more than three months for me to pull off a preliminary fifteen-minute telephone interview with the man. Times were set and then canceled, again and again, because being Mr. Las Vegas keeps Newton pretty busy. (In addition to the in-town shows he performs, his road schedule has, in the past two months alone, taken him to venues in Niagara Falls, Ontario; North Myrtle Beach, South Carolina; Hollywood, Florida; Columbus, Georgia; Cabazon, California; and Wendover, Nevada.)

To his credit, Newton gave it his all when that short phone conversation finally happened—apparently a hallmark of his lotta-bang-for-the-buck stage act. He was effusive about the tour possibilities. He offered a quick geography lesson about how the mountains that ring the city had for years limited growth. He explained the evolution of Vegas from a gambling capital to "an entertainment-based city" where gaming, has slipped to fourth place as an attraction, behind stage acts, restaurants, and shopping. He talked at length about the evolving trends in entertainment, from the Rat Pack singers to the magicians to the comedians and the impersonators to the modern-day circus shows.

He recalled with great irony how "the NBC affiliate came up for sale here in the mid-1970s and Dick Clark, a friend of mine, suggested that he and I buy the station. He checked it out for two months, and when I finally called him to ask about it, he said he'd decided to pass. The opinion was that Las Vegas wasn't going to last."

The sixty-four-year-old Newton seemed genuinely excited about showing off his hometown, dropping tantalizing hints about Howard Hughes's secret tunnels at the Desert Inn. He even suggested that we meet Claudine Williams, whom he described as "my adopted mother" and said had helped build the first Holiday Inn on the Strip, now the site of Harrah's.

"She's in her eighties," he said. "She actually came out here from Texas as a dealer. She knows more about that kind of history than anyone I know."

Newton reserved a special mention for the New Frontier hotel and casino, which opened as the Last Frontier in 1942. Newton said it "probably offers the best history of the town." The sparkle-creep of new Las Vegas had "totally engulfed" the venerable Frontier, Newton said, and "it's probably only a matter of time before it's imploded." When a date for our tour was finally set—after several more failed attempts—I didn't hesitate. I booked a room at the Frontier.

As it turned out, it was as close to historic Las Vegas as I would get.

Despite its endless shimmer, Las Vegas does not encourage reflection. The entire city seems designed to keep visitors from thinking too much. Unless you're in a place where you're gambling or spending money, there's really nowhere to sit. Sidewalks and elevated crosswalks along the Strip are not direct routes from one place to another, but meandering paths that parade you past the endless retailers. It's the rare hotel that doesn't require you to traverse the infinite, Pavlovian clamor of a casino to get to your room.

And once there, well, who has time to reflect when the Frontier's porn channels are free?

If that venerable hotel is the essence of historic Las Vegas, then history here smells vaguely of stale cigarettes and Paco Rabanne. In contrast to the Wynn Las Vegas, towering in tasteful desert shades directly across Las Vegas Boulevard (and boasting both Ferrari and Maserati showrooms right on the premises), the Frontier's main marquee promotes rooms from $44.95, frozen margaritas for $1.99, "the only Bingo on the Strip," and an *Urban Cowboy*–era Gilley's nightclub featuring "Cold Beer . . . Dirty Girls" mud wrestling, and midnight "Bikini Bull Riding." At the Wynn, the registration desk overlooks a magnificent artificial forest and waterfall and features stunning arrangements of fresh-cut flowers. The Frontier's registration desk resembles the checkout line at Costco.

My cellphone rang as I walked the cacophonous miles between the front desk and my room. I answered, and I wasn't particularly surprised to hear there was a snag.

Newton was canceling again. The night before, Mr. Las Vegas had injured his knee while taping his E! network reality show, *The Entertainer*, in Los Angeles. Nasty stuff, according to his assistant. Blown meniscus. Possible surgery. Head fogged by painkillers. Hope you understand.

And so the officially sanctioned Wayne Newton Tour of Historic Las Vegas was not to be. I was reduced to waiting out the hours before my return flight at the Frontier. I spent the time rereading a landmark 1966 *Esquire* story—headline: "Frank Sinatra Has a Cold"—hoping to emulate Gay Talese's deft handling of an elusive star (eventually concluding that I'm no Gay Talese, and that Wayne Newton is no Frank Sinatra), and driving around the perimeter of once-remote Casa de Shenandoah like a stalker, wondering what was going on behind the ten-foot-high block walls and gilded gates that shield Mr. Las Vegas from the gas station, tattoo parlor, Jack in the Box, and other commercial blight that has spread to his doorstep.

And during that excursion, an obvious truth hit me: Historic Las Vegas doesn't really exist—at least not in any form that you can actually tour. (OK, you can see a sampling of artifacts and structures from the pioneer days at the tiny Clark County Museum, which drew thirty-five thousand visitors in fiscal 2005–2006. The Liberace Museum does better, enticing about seventy thousand annually, but neither figure is particularly impressive in a city awash in almost forty million yearly visitors.)

Occasionally you can spot glimpses of history scattered about town, including the bright-red landmark Klondike hotel and casino that squats at the south end of the Strip, fenced off and abandoned since late June (and, I suspect, still reeking of cigarettes and Paco Rabanne). But when I thought back to my fifteen-minute phone conversation with Mr. Las Vegas, it was clear that he had been groping for possibilities, trying to think of where, exactly, historic Las Vegas might be found.

The Desert Inn, site of the reclusive Hughes's aerie? Gone, he had said, replaced by the Wynn. Those secret tunnels? "I'm not sure they exist anymore, but I can show you where they were." He'd mentioned an old equestrian center, then quickly added that he thought it might be "part of the Trump development now."

I'd asked him to name people and places in town where the old Vegas and the new Vegas were colliding in poignant or interesting ways. A favorite old diner consumed by the metastasizing city? A blacksmith for his Arabians who can no longer afford to do business there? The questions seemed to stump him.

When I was back in L.A., I called the recovering Newton and tested my no-tangible-history theory.

"It's funny," he said. "I realized that the only places I could have shown you that truly represented old Las Vegas were the Frontier and the Stardust."

With the closing of the Stardust on Wednesday, only the Frontier remains.

Asked what that said about history in his hometown, Newton said it showed the impact of the transition to corporations from individual owners. Before, he continued, gaming laws limited the number of casinos that could be in the hands of a single owner. With corporations, "there is no one person on the gaming licenses," and so growth is inevitable and seemingly unlimited.

"In Las Vegas, it's what's important now," he said. "And with the corporations able to build these megacities, what *was* doesn't matter to anybody anymore. It's just melted snow."

Even the people who lived Las Vegas's history are waving the white flag. "There's an old-timers club that has met for years," Newton said. "They're all people who have been living here for forty years or more," including Claudine Williams. He said the club recently held its final meeting: "They wanted to have it at the Stardust before it was imploded."

So, then, history in Las Vegas is what happened yesterday. The Desert Inn and its secrets are just memories. The now-closed Stardust is expected to be razed early next year, making way for the city's Next Big Thing, Boyd Gaming Corp.'s splendiferous four-billion-dollar Echelon Place. The Klondike is a slate that soon will be wiped clean, and in its place there will be a 900-room hotel, 1,200 condos, and a casino seven times larger than the original. The funky Frontier is a stubborn rock in a rushing river, but someday soon it too may wash away.

Now Mr. Las Vegas has a bad knee, and all things considered, it's hard not to worry about the way Vegas treats its aging legends.

POSTSCRIPT

This essay is adapted from one that appeared in the November 5, 2006, issue of West, *the magazine of the* Los Angeles Times. *The Frontier hotel closed July 16, 2007, and was demolished four months later. But Newton's stage career continues, though according to a 2015 report in the* Las Vegas Sun, *he last performed in his hometown in April 2010. His headline-making appearances in recent years mostly involved a legal dispute over control of Casa de Shenandoah, which in 2015 he opened as a museum containing personal memorabilia collected during his decades in the spotlight. "But the viability of his museum, in today's Las Vegas, is hardly a certainty," wrote John Katsilometes in the* Sun *story. "A similar attraction dedicated to Liberace closed in November 2010, in large part because Liberace's name recognition had waned. Even Elvis isn't a sure thing in Las Vegas. Cirque du Soleil's 'Viva Elvis' closed and there has been a lackluster response to 'The Elvis Experience' stage show at the Westgate, though 'Graceland Presents Elvis: The Exhibition,' a museum and tour, still is flourishing." Newton told the* Sun *writer he recognized the risk of opening a museum celebrating himself: "I'd be naïve to think otherwise," he said of its long-term viability. "It happens to all of us, but the difference between Casa de Shenandoah and Graceland, for that comparison, is that I am still here. I can boost interest personally if need be." But time respects no legend. Or as one unkind reader wrote in the comments section of that online story: "Good luck Mr. Las Vegas! Maybe you can now focus on suing the plastic surgeons that made you look like a Muppet."*

Chapter Two

Extinction Along Interstate 10

How a 250-ton, steel-reinforced desert dino dream disappeared (2005)

THE FIRST TIME I SAW THE DINOSAURS OF CABAZON, LOOMING LIKE A kitschy desert mirage on the north side of Interstate 10 just outside Palm Springs, I was a young news reporter racing to cover the Liberace death-watch. Despite the urgency of my mission that day—grim reports leaking from behind the compound walls, tearful fans keeping vigil outside, a tabloid reporter already hauled away for attempted trespassing—I eased onto the freeway shoulder and spent a few minutes studying a creation that, to me, conveyed something profound and elemental about Southern California.

Back then, in 1987, the two dinosaurs rose nearly unobstructed from the desert floor. What struck me most was the clear sense of purpose that apparently had set them there, in that desolate spot. There's just nothing unintentional about two hundred fifty tons of steel-reinforced concrete fashioned into the shapes of a one-hundred-fifty-foot-long Apatosaurus ("Dinney") and a sixty-five-foot-tall tyrannosaurus rex ("Rex"). Someone had decided to build them, and in precisely that spot, for some unfathomable reason.

These things happen. The Watt's Towers, Simon Rodia's improbable art project in urban Los Angeles, were no accident, and like the dinosaurs, they had no clear purpose, commercial or otherwise. Of course, everyone knows about Rodia and his towers—the singular and profound result of one man's obsession. But who built the dinosaurs? And why dinosaurs? And why way out in the desert?

You already know how the Liberace story turned out. Legends aren't always built to last. But even as I made my way toward that unfolding desert drama, I couldn't shake the notion that, somewhere out there in that vast, arid weirdness, an even better story was just waiting to be told.

Claude K. Bell was ninety-one when I invited myself into his life. I'd tracked him down through public records, then telephoned his wife, Anna, who at the time was a spry seventy-one. Claude wasn't well, she explained, but if I came out to the desert, and he was feeling up to it, I might be able to talk to him for a little while.

I met him in his studio, just behind the dinosaurs, not far from the Wheel Inn restaurant. It was midsummer, a dry inferno of a day, but the inside of Bell's studio was dim and cool. He received me while sitting stiffly in his rocking chair. He was clearly frail. By then I already knew there were other problems. For years, he had welcomed visitors to the viewing platform in Rex's mouth—the one recreated for that famous scene in the film *Pee-wee's Big Adventure*—and the sliding board down his tail. He'd also built a small gift shop in Dinney's belly. But on the day I met Bell, the whole operation was shut down. The hired caretaker had broken a hip, and Bell's family was trying to decide what to do.

"I think we could go on if we found the right person, someone who understands," Anna told me that day. "Right now we're . . . trying to hang onto this for him, but we just can't get it together enough to do what he wanted to do."

What Claude Bell wanted to do, essentially, was the same thing most of us want to do: make a permanent mark before leaving this world. But as he and his family told his story, Bell's attempt to make his mark struck me as particularly poignant.

He grew up in Atlantic City, New Jersey, where he spent much of his youth creating sand sculptures for the loose change tourists would dig from their pockets. He got so good that for a while he made a career of it, touring the continent creating sand sculptures for fairs and exhibitions. During those years, Bell spent his days building things that had all the

Claude Bell in front of the steel skeleton of Dinney, March 23, 1970, by John Malmin

permanence of smoke. By day's end, what he had created usually was reduced to piles of nothing.

That Sisyphean sense of impermanence apparently wears on a man. "He got tired of working on something for others, then seeing it torn down with no appreciation for its demise," his wife told me. "He said he was going to build something that nobody could tear down."

Bell eventually found permanent employment as a sculptor at Knott's Berry Farm and began raising his family in Buena Park. In 1945 he bought sixty acres of desert land, and it was there that he spent much of his free time. "I kept thinking, 'Why would anyone want to buy a piece of sand and dirt?'" Anna recalled. "I couldn't imagine what he was ever going to do with that piece of ground. But he never regretted it. He'd come out here and look at it and say, 'That's where I'm going to build my dinosaur.'"

Interstate 10 was brand new when the steel skeleton of Dinney began to take shape in the mid-Sixties. By then Bell, too, was in his mid-sixties, even older when he started work on Rex. He had a financial stake in the Wheel Inn, and he imagined his dinosaurs as a reliable magnet for passing motorists with an appetite. But making money was hardly Bell's prime motivation. (He eventually spent about three hundred thousand dollars and countless hours building the dinosaurs, but charged only fifty cents' admission for adults, twenty-five cents for kids between ten and fourteen, and nothing for kids under ten.) No, this clearly was about something else.

And so they rose, two dinosaurs marooned in that godforsaken place. And there they have remained, silent testimony to their creator's pluck and to this land of infinite possibilities. Didn't most of us, after all, come here to build our dinosaurs?

At one point during my visit, Claude Bell leaned forward in his rocking chair and gestured at a piece of plywood leaning against his studio wall. On it, he had sketched plans for a third creature, a mastodon. "You've got to work from the inside out," he said. "It's kind of tricky getting around them." He conceded that a mastodon "isn't in view at this time," but even at ninety-one, he wasn't entirely ruling it out.

Before I left that day, Anna flipped through a scrapbook of photographs of her husband's sculptures. "All these things you see here were torn down," she said. "There's only a few things left."

The biggest of those stood just outside, massive, unmovable, as permanent as one man could make them. Bell's partner in the Wheel Inn, who'd helped assemble Dinney's steel skeleton, predicted the dinos would be structurally sound for at least five hundred years, and at one point Anna bragged, "They'd need a bulldozer and then something to get them down."

And I remember wanting to congratulate their creator for actually doing what so many of us want to do, for leaving a mark. But by then Claude Bell was asleep in his chair. And six weeks later, the man who built the Cabazon dinosaurs was dead.

Here's the thing about Southern California: Permanence is illusion. Legends wither. The past impedes the future. And so, sad to say, Claude Bell's mighty dinosaurs have practically disappeared in the nearly two decades since they first caught my eye.

Oh, they're still there, standing strong and proud as ever on the same patch of desert. But Bell's family eventually sold the sixty acres and the dinosaurs to an Orange County developer who wanted to make a mark of his own. In conjunction with a Christian group, the developer decided to use the dinosaurs as massive roadside billboards to help sell the biblical notion that life on Earth was a divine creation during God's one productive week rather than the result of millions of years of evolution. Bell's dinosaurs have found gainful employment as proselytizers.

But at the same time, the dinosaurs have fallen into a modern version of a tar pit. First came a two-story Burger King, which rose between the dinosaurs and the interstate and partially blocked them from motorists' view. Another restaurant went up, as did a gas station. The dinosaurs seemed to get smaller, sinking deeper and deeper into a commercial swamp that Bell never envisioned. The most thrilling way to see them these days is in satellite photographs. The last time I drove past, I was so distracted by the traffic around the nearby outlet malls and the new twenty-seven-story casino resort that rises into the desert sky like a Kubrick monolith, I didn't even notice the concrete creatures that once so fascinated and inspired me.

The moment struck me later as both sad and inevitable. Anyone with a dream can make their mark here. Few marks, though, are big enough to endure.

POSTSCRIPT

This essay is adapted from one that originally appeared in the November 27, 2005, issue of the Los Angeles Times Magazine. *The commercial creep that was well underway in 2005 continues to surround Claude Bell's two dinosaurs, though a few things have changed. Admission now is $8.95 for adults and $7.95 for children older than two. The owners claim on the site's Facebook page that they "have over fifty dinosaurs, a dinosaur dig, gemstone and fossil panning, and you can climb inside the movie famous Mr. Rex!" One critic noted, however, that he "drive[s] by here every day and I'm still waiting for the other 48 dinos to come out and play." The comment compelled the owners to admit to a bit of hyperbole, conceding that the others actually were in a small exhibit behind Mr. Rex. Another critic lamented, "Sadly, these charming icons* *are currently owned by nitwit 'creationist' types who teach that man and dinosaur coexisted some ten thousand years ago. Apparently, stupidity is alive and well in Cabazon." It's worth noting that Claude Bell's name does not appear on the current owner's website or Facebook page.*

CHAPTER THREE

Looking for Big George Coyle

Love, loss, and the inexorable march of time at Orange County, California's Sea Breeze Pet Cemetery (2015)

THE PHOTO OF BIG GEORGE COYLE'S REMARKABLE HEADSTONE WAS buried deep in the archive at First American Financial Corp. in Santa Ana. I had been browsing for something else when I came across a trove of 1972 images by photographer Henry C. Koerper. He'd photographed a number of the gravesites at the Sea Breeze Pet Cemetery in Huntington Beach, including a joint plot shared by a skunk named Pew and a chipmunk named Dale.

Delighted to discover that Sea Breeze was still in business, I contacted Brenda Pulley, the cemetery's president, to arrange a visit. Why? To be honest, it called to mind Evelyn Waugh's wonderful evocation of a pet cemetery called the Happier Hunting Ground in his 1948 novel *The Loved One*. I also was inspired by *Gates of Heaven*, a 1978 documentary film about pet cemeteries by a then-unknown Errol Morris, his first. (Roger Ebert: "I have seen this film perhaps thirty times, and am still not anywhere near the bottom of it: All I know is, it's about a lot more than pet cemeteries.")

I wanted to visit Sea Breeze myself.

The three and a half acres along Beach Boulevard are a relic hemmed in by commercial clutter, including mattress and tire stores, a Walgreens, a

This 1972 photograph of "Big George" Coyle's grave marker was shot by Henry C. Koerper at Sea Breeze Pet Cemetery, Huntington Beach, California.
FROM A COLLECTION ARCHIVED AT FIRST AMERICAN FINANCIAL CORP. IN SANTA ANA, AND USED WITH PERMISSION

Carl's Jr., a Coldwell Banker office building, and a hulking, new three-story Hoag Health Center. The cemetery first welcomed the public in 1961, back when Beach was one of the county's most significant traffic arteries and this was a relatively quiet lot just a couple miles off the coast. The perpetual invitation to enter comes from an understated blue sign.

The first question that strikes me as I steer into the driveway is: "How many other businesses in Orange County have stayed essentially unchanged for more than half a century?" The second: "Where among the approximately thirty-five thousand occupied plots might I find Big George's headstone?"—the one that includes a photo etching of the well-trained cat squatting self-consciously on a white porcelain toilet?

Overshadowing those questions, though, is the simple fact that such a place still exists in modern Orange County. It's damned rare to find something original here, something besides the mountains that hasn't been eroded by our relentless impulse to grow, change, and evolve. Sea Breeze has been offering funeral services for pets since the Kennedy administration, and that strikes me as significant.

Here's a timeworn place to which tens of thousands of local families have turned while grieving the death of an animal they adored. They've paid serious money for the privilege of interring their companions in these small, well-tended plots. Some have sprung for the roomy whole-body real estate, sold in three- and four-foot-wide parcels excavated to forty-five inches deep to accommodate three and sometimes four stacked caskets. Others have opted for cremation and often burial at the bottom of a square-foot-size, thirty-five-inch-deep shaft that offers stacking space for up to eight containers.

In Orange County's vast and ever-changing landscape, the graves and markers at Sea Breeze are existential anchors. Our pets will die. We will die. Eventually, our descendants will die or move away. But right here, sunk into this earth, are these little attempts at immortality, permanent remembrances of so many Stinkys and Goofys and Crackers, so many Scooters and Fluffers and Porkys onto which we've projected ourselves and everything we hold dear. Many of the Sea Breeze headstones include not just our surnames but the religious iconography of our respective faiths, including the cross that marks the plot shared by Ralf and Charlie Sullivan, and little Cupcake Rosenfeld's poignant Star of David.

The proprietors of Sea Breeze acknowledge the possibility of change. "Oh, they sent someone over to talk about buying the property," says Pulley, nodding over her shoulder at the gleaming Hoag Health Center next door. "But they wanted us to relocate the pets, which would have meant notifying all the owners. They left and never came back."

But isn't change inevitable, especially in ever-developing Orange County? Of course it is. But I also was relieved to hear that the proprietors of Sea Breeze have a plan.

I conveyed to Pulley my rough calculations based on figures she supplied: With between fifteen hundred and two thousand plots left, mostly in what now is the front lawn, and at the current rate of about five new burials per month, I guessed that Sea Breeze has only about twenty-five years before it runs out of these teeny pieces of prime commercial real estate. Wouldn't those three and a half acres then stop producing revenue? Wouldn't it then be smart to sell it to someone looking to develop Sea Breeze into something with a brighter revenue-producing future?

Pulley shakes her head. "We can still bury in existing plots," she says. "And we'll still do cremations. Sea Breeze lives off cremations, thank God."

Pulley says she has no specific plans to sell the property, and even if she does, the new owner would have to jump through a lot of hoops—including public hearings—to use it as anything but a pet cemetery. Considering the fresh flowers, balloons, pinwheels, and chew toys regularly left on Sea Breeze gravesites, you can almost hear the cries of an outraged citizenry.

Besides, the buyer might want to think long and hard about changing anything, since selling pet gravesites and all that goes with it can be lucrative. Pulley downplays this—"It's a good business, not a great business"— but the numbers are intriguing. Casket-plot combos go for between $775 and $935, depending on size. Cremations cost $80 for cats, and $150 for a Lab-size dog. And of course, there's still money to be made selling the $120 extra-large metal urns; $105 "exotic wood" ones; the satin-lined caskets like the ones on the wall display just inside the front door that sell for between $120 and $250; and stone grave markers that go for $275 to $850, the most expensive being the heartbreakers with a photo engraving.

That's good news, too, for Sea Breeze employees who have worked there for decades. Benjamin Gonzalez, the cremator, has been on the payroll for forty-two years. Miguel Cerda, who builds the caskets, about the same length of time. His son, Antonio, has worked here since 2000, tending the grounds. Clem Beld, the eighty-four-year-old driver who picks up deceased pets, has worked for Sea Breeze for nearly twenty years, as has Lisa Stadler, who handles the office with Pulley.

At least for now, no one at Sea Breeze is much worried about job security.

Asked to help locate the plot of Big George Coyle, Pulley retrieves an ancient record from her computer system, prints it out, and leads me along the main path to section five, row eighteen, plot five, in the back right sector of the cemetery. Big George, it turns out, is buried in the cats-only section. "The cat people didn't want any dogs allowed," says Pulley. "They don't like dogs."

Time and weather have worn away the fine details of the etching on his headstone. The porcelain they used back then broke or wore away with age, leaving the marker with an undistinguishable photo. "Kind of sad," Pulley says.

Lost, too, are the details of Big George's remarkable toilet training. I hungered for more from the Sea Breeze records, but at this point I can conclude only two things from the available information: The Studio City phone number for his owner, Elsa Coyle, no longer is in service, and Big George was nineteen years old when he passed.

As remarkable as that is, even nineteen years reminds me that we're all just blips in time. I wonder where Elsa is now. I wonder if she had children or grandchildren who remember her remarkable cat, and if eventually his headstone will be the only evidence that there once was a Big George Coyle. I wonder, too, if I'll be the last person to ever visit Sea Breeze with him in mind. With his family dispersed and his headstone eroded, who's left to marvel at a cat that pooped like a proper gentleman?

POSTSCRIPT

This essay is adapted from one that originally appeared in the July 2015 issue of Orange Coast *magazine. As of 2016, Sea Breeze Pet Cemetery continues to operate along busy Beach Boulevard in Huntington Beach, California, and Big George's eroded headstone remains among the tens of thousands of others available for public viewing.*

CHAPTER FOUR

The Fall and Rise of a Guitar Hero

Some people crash and burn. Dick Dale—Southern California's "King of the Surf Guitar"—crashed and bounced. Five times. There's a lesson in that. (2001)

IT OCCURS TO ME NOW, MANY YEARS LATER, THAT I DIDN'T SO MUCH meet Dick Dale on that grim June day in 1986 but rather was sucked into the eccentric orbit of a flickering rock 'n' roller. It's also obvious, looking back, that I met the "King of the Surf Guitar" at one of the lowest points of his often-calamitous life. On that day, a quarter century after Dale's fame had peaked in *Life* magazine and on *The Ed Sullivan Show*, a rumbling avalanche of poor choices and bad luck—love, money, real estate, career, everything—seemed to finally catch up with him.

I'd called Dale after noticing a brief news item that described the possibility of his eviction from a seventeen-room mansion in Newport Beach, California. New to the state from Pittsburgh, the nonsurfing capital of the world, I knew nothing of surf music or the man *Guitar Player* magazine considers—along with Eric Clapton, Pete Townsend, Jerry Garcia, and Jimi Hendrix—among the "30 Players Who Changed the Way We Sound." Nor did I know anything about the complex series of misfortunes that had led Dale to the edge of the abyss. But the king was losing his castle and, on the surface, his descent into debt seemed like a good morality tale—a fading guitar hero at the end of his rocket ride. I wanted to write about his crash, to sift the debris for any lessons it might hold, and he agreed.

That was my first clue that things aren't always what they seem.

We met for the first time a week or so later in the hallway of an Orange County court. His long, unnaturally black hair was pulled into a ponytail, and he was dressed in the clothes of a lifelong performer, despite a receding hairline and the start of a pizza paunch. Onstage, Dale is known for his power and commanding presence—he's been called a "sonic beast"—but at that moment he looked like an inappropriately dressed forty-nine-year-old man who'd been clocked in the forehead with a metal pipe.

A judge had just upheld a creditor's right to evict him from his three-story dream house near the fabled Wedge at the tip of Balboa Peninsula, a house as much a part of Dale's public persona as his glittery gold Fender Stratocaster. He didn't have time to talk, he said; after months of legal wrangling, the court had given him until the next day to empty the home of his possessions and get out. He was twenty-four hours from being homeless.

"You'll need help," I said, and he was in no position to decline my offer.

From that ringside seat I watched a man truly in the crucible, and what I saw that day was a lesson I've never forgotten. Though clearly stunned, Dale never once slid into self-pity. Within an hour, he'd taken out a yellow legal pad and made a list of the things he would need to rebuild his life virtually from scratch. The list eventually grew to seventeen items. His first priority was saving the guitars and other instruments, the tools he'd need for the comeback in which he had unswerving confidence. Second came the recording equipment. The clothes came third. His beloved Macintosh computers rated sixth; his surfboards fourteenth. The cash and valuables in his safes were an afterthought, at seventeen.

An hour after that—even as he worked toward the brutal eviction deadline, even as he prepared to move into the road-weary twenty-five-foot RV that would become his home for the next year—Dale already was philosophical. "It's not wrong to become broke, but it's a real bad thing if you become poor," he said. "The difference between being broke and being poor is that when you're poor, you don't have the mental ability to want something and work hard enough to get it. I once made a million dollars a year with my career. I made ten thousand dollars for three minutes' work on *The Ed Sullivan Show* in 1963. It all went to agents, record

This photograph by Mike Burns shows Dick Dale performing at the Middle East Restaurant & Nightclub in Cambridge, Massachusetts, on May 28, 2005.

companies, producers, managers, taxes. It's no big deal. I just ended up starting over again, just like I'm going to do now."

I was remembering Dale's words one day last April as I rolled along the dusty road toward the converted desert airport he calls his "Sky-ranch," near Twentynine Palms, California, where, at sixty-four, he's enjoying the most successful and satisfying days of his life and career. I was thinking, too, about how the best stories develop over time, stories in which character is revealed rather than exposed. Fifteen years ago, I chronicled in unsparing detail the fall of a man who can be, all at once, charming, obnoxious, wise, and comically self-absorbed. What I remember most, though, is the way he responded to a boxer's clear and undeniable choice: Get up off the bloodied canvas, or stay down? Facing a future that promised nothing but years of hard work, impossible odds, and no guarantees, Dick Dale pushed himself off the floor, cleared his head, and started to rise.

Psychologists have long been fascinated by people who seem better equipped than others to survive the natural and unnatural disasters of life. In a word, those survivors are "resilient," and the search is on for their secret. "What we know about resiliency is limited from the standpoint of research and empirical data," says Elaine Ann Blechman, a professor of psychology at the University of Colorado, Boulder, and an expert on the topic of resiliency. "But I can give you some hints and guesses."

Resilient people, she says, "can be people of any age faced with statistical odds that most people don't overcome. That can be a child faced with a poor family or difficult home life, to somebody at midlife who has a series of reverses in business and marriage. Most people we know succumb to that. They get depressed and give up. But the resilient person is someone who has enough sense of purpose or vision or meaning as an individual to keep going through very, very difficult times. Extremely difficult times. They're people who feel they have something important or some talent to contribute to the world."

I tell Blechman the broad outlines of Dale's story, explaining how at least five times he has survived the potentially devastating hand that life dealt him. The first was when his white-hot Southern California music career was swamped by a shifting tide of public taste. In the early 1960s, when he was being compared to many of the American greats of the day—"a thumping teenage idol who is part evangelist, part Pied Piper, and all success," proclaimed *Life*—the Beatles, the Stones, and other British invaders suddenly eclipsed his act. Just that quick, Dick Dale was yesterday's news.

Then in 1965, Dale, still in his twenties, was found to have rectal cancer, one of the disease's deadliest forms. Without surgery, his doctor told him later, he might have lived only three months more. The ensuing battle relieved him of part of his small intestine and much of the money he made during his peak earning years of 1960, 1961, and 1962. His weight eventually dropped from one hundred fifty-eight to ninety-eight pounds, and he moved to Hawaii expecting to die. He began studying martial arts and credits the lifestyle changes he learned there to salvaging his health.

He switched gears, opening his first nightclub in Riverside in 1968 even though he knew nothing about running a business. Then, two years later, Dale retooled his stage act and took it to Reno, Lake Tahoe, and Las Vegas. Money flowed again and, this time, having learned his lesson, he sank much of it into real estate—a house in Costa Mesa, apartment buildings in Huntington Beach, marina property in Oxnard, a small airport near Fresno.

He began touring again, but in the early 1970s he had a chance to buy a beer bar called the Playgirl Club in Garden Grove. Dale renamed it The Rendezvous and gradually expanded it into an eighteen-thousand-square-foot musical megaplex. With Dale as a regular stage act and many top bands eager to play at the club, The Rendezvous was a huge success. He soon opened Rendezvous II in Huntington Beach. By the mid-1970s, things were going so well that he jumped at the chance to buy the magnificent mansion at the tip of Balboa Peninsula originally built in 1926 by razor magnate King Gillette, though he had to sell some of his other properties to afford it.

By then, though, Dale's personal life was unraveling. The fallout from a nasty, protracted, and very public divorce drained him financially and damaged his reputation. The deals he cut to save his beloved mansion put him on the road to financial disaster.

In 1984, Dale spilled a pot of boiling cooking oil on his left leg, left foot, and left hand—his guitar-picking hand. "It was like his hand was melted," remembers Cynthia Huffman, Dale's companion at the time, who now is president of a North Hollywood casting agency. "For a lot of people that wouldn't be tragic, but when you're left-handed and play guitar really, really fast, that's a really big deal. That's how he made his living."

Third-degree burns are among the most painful injuries a human body can suffer, and Dale's recovery at a burn center in Irvine was excruciating. His doctors predicted that the resulting scar tissue would prevent him from playing the guitar, but even then, Huffman remembers, "Dick's attitude was, 'Look at all these poor little kids that were in fires and in so much pain. It could have been worse. How dare me whine about a little hand thing?'"

He said something else then that Huffman still remembers: "If I can't play guitar, we'll figure something else out."

"That's what [resilience] is all about in a way—living large," Blechman says. "Having a sense that life is a finite opportunity. 'I have a life and I'm going to make the most of this. It's a kick to be alive.'"

Celebrating Dick Dale for anything other than his music can be tricky, like celebrating *Hustler* publisher Larry Flynt for defending the First Amendment. In some stories, the hero isn't easy to understand or even like. Dale is an impossibly complicated, often contradictory subject— inseparable from the history of Southern California beach culture, but with an accent that betrays his Massachusetts upbringing; capable of both startling wisdom and laughable lapses of judgment; a self-professed health freak with weaknesses for buttered popcorn and pizza; a nonstop talker who numbers among his favorite sayings, "He who knows does not speak. He who speaks does not know."

So let's start with the music. The guy can play virtually anything— guitar, drums, trumpet, piano, ukulele, accordion, the list seems endless— though his unorthodox way with string instruments makes the violin a logistical nightmare. He's self-taught, which explains why he plays the guitar upside down (to accommodate his left-handedness) and backward, with the heavier strings along the bottom of the guitar's neck and the thinner strings along the top. "If someone tries to sound like Dick, they can't," says Ron Eglit of Huntington Beach, Dale's bass player and friend for the past twenty-three years. "It's because on a physical level they're not playing the same way. He has his own language for music. He's just in a whole 'nother world."

Dale's musical passions are boundless (a Slim Whitman CD was slotted next to a self-made disc of "Arabic music" in his Chevy Suburban's CD rack) and he makes music onstage and in the studio with a striking combination of technical skill and raw instinct. A Southern California beach-culture icon by the early 1960s—his music infuses the 1963 classic "Beach Party" with Frankie Avalon and Annette Funicello—he remains true to his trademark brand of high-decibel instrumental electro-throb.

"In our world he's definitely one of the guys who shaped the way we do things now," says *Guitar Player* magazine editor Michael Molenda. "He's never been considered a technical genius, but he does have an intensely strong personality that comes through in the way he plays. It's passionate and arrogant, but in a good way. He attacks the guitar to squeeze every single aggressive noise possible out of it. He's got this feral energy. Can you imagine that in 1962, with all of that namby-pamby pop of the day? Here comes this guy in surf clothes and he's brutalizing a guitar. He influenced a ton of players."

Another thing: At an age when most people are slowing down, Dale—who does not drink, smoke, take drugs, or eat much red meat—still approaches life and work with the infectious enthusiasm of a hyperactive cheerleader. He doesn't sleep much, preferring catnaps and a four-hour doze during the night. During his waking hours he's a tireless student of life, competent at everything from architectural drawing to operating a road grader. An Air Force veteran (a crash crew member, not a pilot), he got his private pilot's license in 1974 but is no less proud that he poured the cement for every square inch of the nearly three-thousand-foot-long runway on the eighty-one-acre Skyranch. He personally trained the two horses he keeps there to obey his voice commands, just like the lions and other big cats he once kept in the mansion. With his second wife, Jill, a bass player, he's helping teach their nine-year-old son, Jimmy, everything from driving a Massey Ferguson tractor to reading a pilot's map. Jimmy often plays drums onstage with his parents with a sophistication and sense of rhythm that's downright eerie.

Reviewers of his recent stage shows have lapsed into purple hyperbole. "TWO HUGE THUMBS UP!!!!" enthused one; gushed another: "[The man's] musical gift is drawing the hypnotic, sexual power of his songs through his almost lyrical staccato barrage."

But if Dick Dale's earsplitting sound is best appreciated from a distance, then, perhaps, so is the man himself. Dale can be overbearing—"Sometimes I just amaze myself," he says without irony while cranking his latest work on the Suburban's CD player—and that sometimes creates an aura of self-importance that can hover around him like a fog. He's not the only celebrity to speak of himself in the third person, it's just that he doesn't have the cultural gravitas of, say, Muhammad Ali and others who also make it a habit. Despite warnings to Jimmy about bragging, Dale spends a lot of time talking about himself and his influence on music.

Maybe that's a holdover from the early days of his career, when he watched better-marketed surf bands—the Surfaris, the Chantays, the Ventures, the Beach Boys—rise to national prominence. Despite being hailed at the time as a fleet-fingered guitar magician and one of rock's true originals, only one of his five local hits, "Let's Go Trippin'," ever broke into *Billboard*'s national top one hundred. In 1961 it climbed to number sixty.

"We needed marketing, because word of mouth ain't gonna take you nationwide," Dale says now. "We didn't do it."

Perhaps to compensate, the amazing Dick Dale generates an equally amazing amount of Dickocentric blather. It accumulates like drifting snow, and as it does, it's easy to forget that, during the past fifteen years he's done that rarest of things: exactly what he said he was going to do.

Too often in the media, years of hard work weigh less than fifteen minutes of fame. Want proof? Search the *Los Angeles Times* archives to find out whose name appeared more often during the past three years, Gao Xingjian, last year's Nobel laureate in literature (twenty-three), or

Darva Conger, the winning contestant on *Who Wants to Marry a Multi-Millionaire?* (eighty-nine).

Maybe that's why I want so badly to revisit Dick Dale's story. Having chronicled his fifteen minutes of infamy in 1986, it's a chance to make sure that they don't overshadow what has happened since. Turns out, the most interesting chapters of his story unfolded far from the public eye.

Dale and I lost touch sometime in the late 1980s. I embarked on a novel-writing career that promised, well, nothing but years of hard work, impossible odds, and no guarantees. During those years, watching from afar, I was regularly inspired by news accounts of Dale chipping away at the improbable.

After hearing his name in a radio report this spring, I e-mailed him congratulations about the upcoming release of his new CD, "Spatial Disorientation." He replied with a burst of electronic joy: "So much to share with you of a positive light . . . my son Jimmy plays drums and is now playing like a madman . . . we're doing a concert together raising money for the church and kids in our little town of Twentynine Palms. The Dick Dale family, my wife Jill, Jimmy and me . . . it's like Mayberry here. I love it, plus I have my own airport. Check my Web page, dickdale.com, and read all the good fun things that working around the clock brings."

And so I set out to reconnect with Dick Dale. To finish the story.

After making his priority list in 1986, he began a slow, steady climb. As he had done for years, he approached each day with a mix of Buddhist philosophy, Catholic resolve, Protestant work ethic, and the studied nonchalance of a laid-back Southern California surfer. "Wherever I am is where I'm at," he often says. "I learned that from being around animals and watching the way they deal with things. They deal with what's happening at that moment, then they decide what's next. Like Einstein said, there's a formula for everything, so why make a big deal out of it?"

There's a good chance Einstein never said anything like that, but Huffman says that attitude is pure Dick Dale. "Even though he's as complex as he is—I think there's, like, five of him—he's really very simple and stays true to that one idea: 'If it's broke, I don't have time to worry. Just fix it and move on, and it's up to me to fix it.'"

Within a year of his eviction, he'd recorded a version of the classic surf tune "Pipeline" with Stevie Ray Vaughan that got him a 1987 Grammy nomination, his first. (He no doubt was the only nominee that year who was living in an RV in his parents' driveway at the time the nominated song was recorded.) He bought a house in Garden Grove, refurbished it, and sold it for a profit. He bought another, as well as some property in Twentynine Palms. He also bought an airplane to replace the one he'd lost during his divorce and, at that point, he says, "My dream was to have my own airport."

He eventually fell in love with both Jill and the high desert, and they set up camp far from the Pacific coast where, several lifetimes before, he'd been king. The song "Nitro," from his *Tribal Thunder* CD, hit big on alternative radio stations in 1993, and he became what surely was the oldest red-hot act on the college grunge circuit. By the time the film *Pulp Fiction* was released in 1994—it opened with the blitzkrieg sound of Dale's classic "Misirlou" and sent a new generation of music fans scouring the film's credits: Who *was* that guy?—his resurrection was well underway.

The *Pulp Fiction* soundtrack went triple platinum, selling more than three million copies in the United States. Dale eventually started his own record company, Dick Dale Records, and began doing everything himself—recording, distribution, promotion, booking, contracts. With a fan's help, he built his own website. Last I checked, more than a quarter-million web surfers had visited the site. His CDs started moving faster. Endorsement deals followed. Dale's tunes started turning up in television commercials, everything from Domino's Pizza to Mountain Dew to Nissan to Barclay's Bank of London. He did the talk-show circuit—Rosie, Conan, Dave. He has toured internationally and is just wrapping up a cross-country club tour that will bring him to the Coach House in San Juan Capistrano on July 6 and the Roxy Theatre in West Hollywood on July 7.

Less than a decade after losing everything, Dick Dale is bigger than he's ever been.

I'm driving the straight, dusty road that leads to Dale's Skyranch, to the happy place that represents a life rebuilt.

He lives on a high-desert plain once used as an emergency airfield for the nearby Marine base, then later as a staging area for a religious organization's relief flights. From a distance, the ranch looks like a heavy-equipment storage yard. The house isn't much, a far cry from the mansion, and not even as nice as the rambling seven-thousand-square-foot home he designed and built for his aging parents just a few miles away. It's surrounded by a grown man's toys: two backhoes, a road grader, a water tanker, a twenty-six-foot scissors lift, a dune buggy with flat tires, four motorcycles, three four-wheel all-terrain vehicles, two tractors, and two RVs, including the one he called home during his post-mansion exile. He calls it his "anchor," always there, just in case.

He greets me in a battered golf cart that looks like something out of a golf-themed *Road Warrior* sequel. Out here, appearances don't matter. Dale's a bit heavier, a bit balder, talkative as ever but a little wary. Life is good, he says. Time is money. He doesn't need publicity. He's supposed to be getting ready for a summer tour and finishing work on the new CD, which he'll release in August, or whenever he's good and ready now that he's running the show at Dick Dale Records.

Still, he wants to show me around the new world he's built. I'm an enthusiastic tourist. Having watched him put his foot on the bottom rung of the ladder, it's good to see him here.

He tells me how he and Jill met, and how amazing Jimmy was from the day he was born. He shows videos as proof—Jimmy working his drum set like a pro, Jimmy in his martial arts outfit breaking a pine board with his tiny fist, Jimmy kicking serious butt during a tae kwon do championship. He shows me how, using the stress breaks every twenty feet along his concrete runway, he taught Jimmy to count in increments of twenty. Dale points to the roof of his house and one of the outbuildings, explaining that he just put a thirty-year shingle on both, then a twenty-year protective coating on top of that.

"I want to be buried here," he says, and clearly, to him, Skyranch is more than just a place.

I take it all in as we ease down the runway, remembering a moment toward the end of that frenzied twenty-four-hour pre-eviction marathon in 1986. With twenty minutes left before the marshals arrived, Dale grabbed a shovel and went to his small patio garden. He'd once planted a mango seed, and through the years it had grown into a small tree. Whenever Dale moved on, the mango tree always moved with him. As he dug that day, he explained that the task of uprooting it got harder each time, but that it always survived.

It was the perfect metaphor for the resilience I sensed in Dale, and my story back then ended on a hopeful note by recounting the tale of the king's sacred mango tree. It was quite lovely. It was also, perhaps, a bit too gauzy.

"Whatever happened to the mango tree?" I ask, fully expecting it to be flowering, like its owner, out here in the brown-gray Twentynine Palms lunarscape. But Dick Dale shakes his head. It didn't survive the trauma.

Some things, I suppose, are just hardier than others.

POSTSCRIPT

This essay is adapted from one that originally appeared in the June 17, 2001, issue of the Los Angeles Times Magazine. *Dale continued to tour for more than a decade after it appeared, and, in 2015 when Dale was 78,* Billboard *magazine reported that "Dale's health concerns have become an unlikely viral sensation following the wide dissemination of a July 29 interview for the* Pittsburgh City Paper *that had the guitar hero declaring: 'I can't stop touring because I will die. Physically and literally, I will die.' [His] road regimen has less to do with the love of satisfying oldies hounds and Quentin Tarantino fans . . . than with paying medical bills involving diabetes, post-cancer treatment, and other debilitating conditions. Suddenly, he's the poster child for a generation that's not too sick to work, but too sick to retire."*

CHAPTER FIVE

Lesbian Cairn Terrier Owners, Unite!

Pagans and witches and knitters, oh my. We're all out there, sifting our-selves into ever-smaller subatomic clusters on social networking sites. In the process, we're also creating an online psychosocial x-ray of Southern California. (2014)

I WAS AT MY HOME COMPUTER SCROLLING THROUGH THE STAGGERING cross-section of humanity on a website called Meetup. Since relocating to the south Orange County community of Laguna Niguel a few months ago, I'd successfully mined the social connection site for fellow soccer players interested in weekly pickup games. But while doing so, I stumbled upon what may be the most perfect spot from which to survey the curious breadth and depth of modern Southern California.

"There's a group called Orange County Lesbian Cairn Terrier Own-ers," I called to my wife, an avid dog walker who also was trying to con-nect. "Three members. They meet once a week in distant Yorba Linda."

Not quite right, we agreed.

"Anything else interesting?" she asked.

Well, *everything*.

The science is pretty solid: Humans are social creatures. We clump together in small, or sometimes massive, affinity groups with others who like the things we do—Catholics, Muslims, and Jews; fans of Spring-steen, Eminem, and Lady Gaga; brand loyalists of Coke, Pepsi, and Dr Pepper; hunters, birdwatchers, vegans; devotees of Bill Maher, Pat

Orange County's Lesbian Cairn Terrier Owners group meets weekly.
PHOTO ILLUSTRATION BY PRISCILLA IEZZI AND MINDY BENHAM OF *ORANGE COAST* MAGAZINE, AND USED WITH PERMISSION

Robertson, Rachel Maddow, and Rush Limbaugh. The lines are permeable—somewhere out there, I'm sure there's a Muslim Limbaugh fan that supports animal rights—but the lines are also pretty reliable. If there are two like-minded souls, there's a good chance they now can find each another, thanks to social connection sites.

Given our impulse to bond, it's not surprising that we continually sift down our relationships into ever-finer gradients. But social networking technology allows us to connect with people on a granular level, quickly locating those who share our specific passions for, say, fellow lesbians who own cairn terriers. Whole industries have sprung up around that ability for hyperspecific questing—dating, used-car shopping, Craigslist classifieds, collector forums, you name it. Even porn websites have evolved into elaborate menus of special interests, often clinically defined.

I'm not entirely sure this is a good thing. I've spent most of my life seeking out people who *aren't* like me, because through them I learn more about the world. Today, some of my most interesting friendships are with ranchers, doctors, and mechanics; swimmers, physicists, and ideologues from both the left and right; cops, cons, and at least a dozen artists who make an enviable living painting ducks. True, the two dozen guys on my regular soccer club came together because of a shared passion for the sport, but I take endless pride in the fact that, at one point, our roster included players from eleven countries of origin.

I'll reserve judgment on the long-term sociological impacts of narrow-casting for friends, because, like this new pope, who am I to judge? I just know that belatedly discovering Meetup was like stumbling into an unseen world that has been operating, day and night, somewhere just off my radar screen for the past ten years.

So who's out there, and what do they do in their spare time? Here's a quick sampling of observations from my Meetup explorations, offered without judgment:

The Orange County Pagans have met 322 times since the group was founded in December 2002. Their organizer is MistressPrime, and their Meetup page says the 190 members are all about pagan and Wiccan fellowship, Earth-based spirituality, witches, druids, and the occult. Of note: They're being out-recruited by the Orange County Witches group, which boasts 233 members. Also of note: MistressPrime turns up as the organizer of the Orange County Pirates Meetup Group, "a place fer ye pirate history enthusiasts and historical re-enactors to swap stories of high-seas adventures and boast about yer booty."

The Orange County Ladies' Social Club, founded in March 2013, has only seven members. Its Meetup page describes the group as a "perfect destination for happy, affluent, stay-at-home wives (aged twenty-one to thirty-five) seeking to form true and lasting friendships with . . . Ivy League alumni, consultants, writers, philanthropists, socialites, housewives, and ladies who lunch." Only "mature, honest, moral, ethical, upstanding, law-abiding, biological female residents of Orange County" need apply. Fair warning: The vetting process for prospective members requires a photo, a background check, and access to social networking accounts such as Facebook, Twitter, and LinkedIn. In addition, a meet-and-greet phone call or videoconference may be required of applicants, who should not be "overly dogmatic about restrictive religious, political, or ultramodern feminist views." Finally: "We will not waste our valuable time, energy, and resources, or soil our reputations by associating with convicted criminals or immoral, unethical people." Its organizer closed an e-mail to me "Impeccably yours," and I still can't tell if she was serious.

The Dana Point–based Beach Cities Scooter Club, by contrast, has cast a much wider membership net since its founding in 2008. "We don't disenfranchise scooterists because of their ride (i.e., CVs versus 'shifters'; Asian versus Italian, etc.), nor do we arbitrarily limit the number of riders at a Meetup event," assures reigning Scootermeister Alan Spears. "Everyone is welcome to join, and ride, regardless of displacement, make, or model. Hell, you needn't even be in the 949 area code!"

The Orange County Fiberistas is a 107-member crochet and knitting group founded in 2007 and "open to all yarn lovers" in the O.C. area. The group's welcome page says, "We are an open community, interested in spreading the joy of all fiber-related addictions," which seems like a pretty straightforward focus compared to the thirty-nine-member Tustin-based Real Bunco Babes of Orange County, which describes its members as women over thirty who want to make friends, have fun, and play Bunco, although, curiously, the group's introductory message mentions wine and potlucks as prominently as it does Bunco.

There's a purity to that, actually, and a pattern. Because as with my soccer team of delusional old men, it's not really about soccer. It's about connecting; there just aren't that many excuses for men my age to hang out together. Most of us pursue personal obsessions because they help us feel part of something bigger than ourselves. Soccer, or Bunco, or yarn, or scooters, or witchcraft—they're all just means to an end in Orange County, where just about everyone is electronically connected to just about everyone else, while seemingly starved for real companionship.

If there's a bottom to the county's deep well of niches, I haven't yet found it. The Orange County I see on Meetup is like a Russian nesting doll—one discovery simply leads to another, on and on, into a seemingly infinite pool of ever-more-intriguing subatomic clusters. The twenty-one goddesses of the Goddess Temple of Orange County have a Meetup group, as do the county's Poles, Canadians, and Boston terrier lovers. Scuba divers? You'll find them topside on the second Wednesday of every month, at the Fuddrucker's in Lake Forest. (Motto: "Dive. Rinse. Repeat.")

I'm glad technology has made it easier for us to connect. But I'm just as thrilled by the chance to peek into those unfamiliar worlds, if only from a distance. The ability to experience such a wide and fascinating swath of our species reminds me that the place where we live is as interesting as anywhere else on the planet, and how lucky we are that it's all close enough to touch.

POSTSCRIPT

This essay is adapted from one that originally appeared in the January 2014 issue of Orange Coast *magazine. I did find a weekly pickup soccer game through Meetup.com and continued to play with that group for several years. Meetup.com and countless other social-interaction websites and apps now available for smartphones and computers continue to connect people of all interests, passions, quirks, and kinks.*

Chapter Six

Are We There Yet?

Two authors, four kids, and a pair of rented minivans on a 6,500-mile, novel-flogging, dream-catching adventure across the Western literary landscape (1998)

WE'RE ROLLING ALONG THE I-10 EASTBOUND, CHASING DESTINY IN A rented minivan. The sun is broiling the hard-pack California desert outside our little bubble, but inside we're more than comfortable. To get ready for our four-week, ten-state, book-flogging odyssey, my two kids supplemented our vehicle's considerable amenities with a few of their own—a cooler full of "snicky-snacks," dual Game Boys, Auto Bingo cards, journals, donated audio books, a CD player, and twenty-five favorite CDs. We are a seventy-five mph, climate-controlled entertainment complex.

More important, we have a box full of my second novel, *Shadow Image*, and a supply of foam-board sales displays featuring its cover, each churned out on an after-school assembly line by nine-year-old Lanie and six-year-old Parker. We have three thousand promotional postcards that I designed and paid for, and a schedule of events organized by an independent publicist I hired to help promote the second in my four-book series of psychological thrillers keyed to the vagaries of human memory.

A quick glance in my rearview mirror lets me know I'm not alone. My friend and fellow author, Philip Reed, is tailing us in a nearly identical minivan with his two sons, Andrew, a twelve-year-old chess master, and Tony, an eight-year-old air-guitar impresario. Phil is promoting *Low*

Rider, the second novel in a "car noir" series published by Pocket Books. The *New York Times* called the first "a volatile concoction of speed, sex and sleaze."

Together, as our wives back home work at the less-risky jobs that sustain our families, we're barnstorming a circuit that will take us from Southern California in a counterclockwise, sixty-five-hundred-mile loop around the West. Along the way, we intend to sign books and read selected passages to anyone who'll listen. We'll pass out free copies to influential booksellers and exploit the novelty of our self-styled Dads Tour to get airtime on radio and feature stories in local newspapers. When things get slow in the larger stores, I'll play my harmonica as loudly as I can to attract a crowd. Silence equals death in our line of work, and we're out to make some noise. We're shedding the mien of serious novelists to become a bookstore version of those human directionals who point giant foam fingers at model homes.

The Dad's Tour participants before their ten-state book flogging odyssey.
PHOTO FROM THE COLLECTION OF MARTIN J. SMITH

This is not exactly what we envisioned when we gave up regular paychecks to spin crime fiction, but reality for newcomers like us is as cold and hard as the bottom line: Critical acclaim is nice, but most publishers bet on sales figures, not kind words. And so we're on the road—Kerouac and Kesey for the Nineties, as one Colorado bookstore owner dubbed us—driving hard toward a dream, bestseller or bust.

"Are we there yet?" my impatient boy asks just forty miles into the trip, and I tell him no, we aren't there yet. He focuses again on his Game Boy. I refocus on the horizon, but his question perches on my shoulder like a mockingbird. The answer is unavoidable: No, I'm not there yet.

Most mystery or crime-fiction writers get just a few chances in which to evolve from a flyspeck on the literary landscape into something approaching a John Grisham, Patricia Cornwell, or Dean Koontz. "Figure you've got five books to make it," Koontz told me after I signed my two-book contract with Jove in 1994. Used to be, he said, publishers gave promising writers time to develop an audience. And even if their books never became bestsellers, those novelists could make a decent living writing so-called midlist books. Today, the midlist has virtually disappeared as the industry risks fewer and fewer dollars on books of modest potential. "There's the top of the list and then there's everything else," says Hillary Cige of Jove, who edited my books. "No one can afford to do little [books] anymore. And the stores just don't support little."

Koontz's five-book estimate seems, in retrospect, wildly optimistic. More than fifty-thousand new titles will be published in the United States this year, about fourteen hundred of them in the broad genre known as mystery or crime fiction. Only a handful will break through to the bestseller lists. Some will get there because they're great books hand-sold by enthusiastic bookstore owners. Others will stink but will get there anyway thanks to huge promotional budgets or an incomprehensible alchemy of topic, timing, and public mood.

Then there are books such as *Shadow Image* and *Low Rider*, which arrive at stores like abandoned children—and, as Phil discovered, sometimes don't arrive at all. Mass-market paperback originals like mine have a life span only slightly longer than that of a mayfly—three to six weeks, during which they're reviewed, recommended by booksellers, and displayed prominently in stores. After that, many stores keep a copy or two, then strip the covers off the rest and ship them back for a refund. If a book's sell-through rate is less than 50 percent, the publisher starts to worry. Your editor wonders what went wrong, and your agent may lose faith. It's brutal, and effective promotion is critical.

"The day I got my author copies of *Bird Dog*, I thought my job was finally done," Phil says of his first novel. "I thought if the reviews were good, I could sit back and the book would sell. But that was the very moment I needed to get my energy back up, to change gears and go out and promote. I realized if I didn't, it might disappear without a trace."

That means shedding the literary-lion persona you projected in your author photograph, armoring yourself with a crush-proof ego, and proceeding with the determination of a door-to-door salesman. "It seems to be almost accepted now in our genre that you're going to promote your own book and you're going to pay for it," says Baltimore novelist Laura Lippman, who this year won crime fiction's top honor, an Edgar Award from the Mystery Writers of America. "And if you're not willing to do it, your publisher interprets it as 'You're not that serious.'"

It helps to know that many best-selling authors, including James Ellroy and Michael Connelly, spent staggering amounts of time and money promoting their work before they earned the loyalty of readers and the marketing support of their publishers. Ellroy, the author of *L.A. Confidential* and other international blockbusters, advised me to pump every cent of my proceeds into promotion, as he once did.

Many crime writers today schmooze booksellers at trade shows and conventions, hawk books on personal websites, pool resources to get the best travel deals. (Jan Burke says she and fellow Long Beach writer Wendy Hornsby once used Southwest Airlines' "Friends Fly Free" program as the basis of a joint promotional tour.) Some authors now hand out home-baked cookies at signings, auction T-shirts, raffle door prizes, wear costumes, or otherwise behave like slicer-dicer hucksters on late-night infomercials. "Mystery writers have shown the rest of the world how to do it," says Dulcy Brainard, mystery forecast editor for the trade magazine *Publishers Weekly*. "It's a testament to their feisty spirit as a group that they didn't waste their time beating their breasts and pulling their hair out, saying, 'Poor me!' They figured out a way to do something about it."

With overwhelming odds against breakout success, many crime writers develop a sort of wartime camaraderie, exchanging contacts at the nation's one-hundred-plus mysteries-only bookstores, sharing the stage at workshops, writing cover blurbs for each other's books. Phil and I met last fall at a mystery convention in Monterey. After speaking together on a panel of first-time novelists, one of whom had spent more than sixty thousand dollars flogging a book for which he received an eight-thousand-dollar advance, we retreated to lunch and decided there had to be an alternative to emptying our bank accounts. We knew that promotion was a do-it-yourself job. But we also knew the commercial and critical performances of our first books had given us a head start. My *Time Release* eventually went into a third printing, and Phil's *Bird Dog* sold out its first printing; both were nominated for crime-fiction awards. The sales of our second books would either move us closer to the dream or further from it.

The solution, we decided, was to do something completely nuts.

When we first arrive at Tucson's Clues Unlimited for the first of more than fifty store and media events, my minivan looks more like a garbage scow than a sophisticated mobile entertainment complex. Maps, fast-food wrappers, and Game Boy cartridges tumble to the pavement every time the doors open. The front grille features the start of a squashed-bug collection that, three weeks later, would prompt someone in San Francisco to note: "Scrape that stuff off, you could make a nice soup." And that was long after my son removed the hummingbird.

Phil, pathologically neat, arrives a few minutes later in a van that looks showroom fresh, Gallant to my Goofus. We are ushered to a table piled high with copies of our books and survey the store. We are, we notice, the only people present who do not actually work there.

"It's this heat," explains Charlene Taylor, one of the store's owners, referring to the 105 degrees outside.

As a crime writer, you are the Master of the Universe. Characters behave as you wish. You reward good, punish evil, dispense justice. But we quickly discovered that as a self-promoter, you control nothing. Our little caravan through the Southwest coincided precisely with what scientists now say was the hottest July since reliable record keeping began. At one southern Colorado store, the resident cat attracts a larger crowd than we do during the ninety minutes we spend disassembling and reassembling our signing pens. Exasperated, we later ask a Barnes & Noble salesclerk in Denver what she feels is the best way to promote a book. "TV," she said. "You know, *Oprah, Good Morning America.* That sort of thing really helps."

Last we checked our messages, neither had returned our calls.

We soldier on, looking ahead to the Pacific Northwest, with its reliable gloom. But the heat wave continues and the turnouts remain thin. We make the best of it, but at night, as we watch our kids cooling down in motel pools, Phil and I ponder whether our literary careers might hinge on something other than our skill at creating memorable characters and fast-paced plots.

We'd realized by then that the infernal hot spell was not the only hindrance. Five days into the trip, Phil noticed an alarming trend on our "drive-by signings"—unscheduled stops to chat with a store manager and sign the books on hand. Though a fixture in the mystery bookstores, the hardcover *Low Rider* often was absent in the big chain outfits. Had someone screwed up the distribution? Had his book been "orphaned" by the untimely departure of its editor, the person who typically champions a book from conception to delivery? Had the chains' centralized ordering staffs simply passed on it?

These are troubling questions when you're halfway into a self-financed, sixty-five-hundred-mile tour, the kids are cranky, your gas credit cards are worn thin, and you've eaten nothing but gorditas for weeks. Besides, it made no sense considering the success of Phil's first book. "The worst thing was, I couldn't get a straight answer out of anyone," he says.

As writers, we were prepared to have our egos battered by critics. As self-promoters, we were willing to become the Barnum & Bailey of American letters. But Phil made a seemingly safe assumption before spending thousands of dollars to promote *Low Rider*—that it would actually be in stores.

Confronted with a problem too large for us to solve, we reconsidered our future one sweltering day in Seattle as we taxied by a Jack in the Box. The sign on the window read, "Ask us about career opportunities," and we thought, "Hmmm."

One evening after two weeks on the road, we saw a vivid demonstration of how outmatched our books were. A segment on CBS's *48 Hours* described how Warner Books—the same publisher that in 1992 made book-marketing history with the widely panned megahit *The Bridges of Madison County*—had launched a megabucks campaign to put Nicholas Sparks's first book on national bestseller lists. The prime-time feature was perfectly timed to boost Sparks's second book onto bestseller lists, and in that strategy I sensed the work of a promotional wizard.

The Dads Tour, on the other hand, sometimes seemed like the work of a sitcom writer. The day before our Clues Unlimited appearance, for example, Phil and I had arranged to call a Tucson radio host from separate pay phones so we could appear together on his talk show. I chose a secluded bank of phones at an elegant resort and admonished my kids to keep absolutely silent while I was on the air. They cooperated beautifully, but just as we went live, a gaggle of preteens paraded into the nearby bathrooms. It sounded like I was calling from prison.

Without my wife's steely sense of law and order, the civilization inside our minivan quickly degenerated into anarchy, *Lord of the Flies* on wheels. At Page One bookstore in Albuquerque, my kids disappeared into the children's section while I spoke to a dozen or so people in the center of the store.

I was deep into my spiel on the unreliability of memory in criminal justice when people started laughing. I turned to find my six-year-old engaged in a spirited puppet show from behind a low wall. Like a rubber-faced Chevy Chase to my somber Jane Curtin, the dragon he'd found was mimicking my every word and gesture.

At a store in Bellingham, Washington, our raucous little horde swarmed through the doors, overwhelming a staff that, until then, had found the Dads Tour idea rather charming. My daughter was doing her best Sarah McLachlan imitation on the store's sound system when a nervous manager snatched the microphone from her hands and urged us to begin our talk.

By then, Phil and I were wondering what possible difference our efforts could make. And yet in that isolated corner of the United States, a thousand miles from home, a stranger came by on a Saturday afternoon and introduced himself. He'd read and enjoyed *Bird Dog*, Phil's first book, and had brought his copy for Phil to sign. He then bought a copy of *Low Rider* and had Phil sign that, too. In our headlong rush toward the dream, we'd lost sight of something real: the passion and reverence that many people still reserve for books. "Seeing that firsthand was enormously gratifying," Phil said later.

Things changed for us that day, and for the rest of the trip through Washington, Oregon, and Northern California, we focused on the journey instead of the destination.

The minivan I'm about to turn in to a rental agent at Long Beach Airport is undamaged but far different from the one my kids and I picked up. We've nearly quadrupled the odometer reading. The front end looks like the fallout of an entomological explosion. In the road dust on the rear window, the names of the Dads Tour survivors are inscribed in our children's scrawl.

"You can't wash it now," Phil had said one day late in the trip. "It's like folk art."

I unload the duffel bags and camping equipment, then drain the cooler. I shovel out the spent batteries and broken kids' meal trinkets. I empty the glove compartment of its lump of maps, TripTiks, and Auto Club travel guides, and place the rental papers into the empty cavern. The last thing I remove is a Native American souvenir that my kids bought in Santa Fe. It had dangled for weeks from the minivan's rearview mirror, an odd assembly of leather, feathers, beads, and webbing called a dream catcher.

According to legend, the night air is filled with dreams. A dream catcher hung just above one's head can capture those dreams. Good dreams slip through a hole at center of the web, and those you get to keep. Bad dreams get tangled in the web and perish with the first light of a new day. The dream catcher instructions say, "Native Americans believe that dreams have magical qualities, the ability to change or direct one's path in life," and I believe that, in many ways, the magic already has worked for me.

But as I close the minivan door for the last time, I wonder if the ancients ever envisioned a chase vehicle quite like this.

POSTSCRIPT

This essay is adapted from one that originally appeared in the November 1, 1998, issue of the Los Angeles Times Magazine. *Smith and Reed continue to write novels and other books (Smith has published five novels and four non-fiction books, including this one, and Reed has published five novels and four nonfiction books). But both also resumed working full-time jobs in February 2000 and continued to work those jobs for the next sixteen years. They still hope to get "there" someday.*

Chapter Seven

The Cinematic Landmark of *Red Asphalt*

Why those epic California Highway Patrol driver's-ed splatter films are among the most watched film franchises ever to come out of California (2006)

As memorable adolescent experiences go, viewing one of the California Highway Patrol's *Red Asphalt* films ranks right up there with your first kiss or having your parents come home early to find a kegger in full swing. For generations, the lights have dimmed, the screen has flickered, and like young Alex in Stanley Kubrick's *A Clockwork Orange*, the state's youngest drivers have been compelled to watch this strange and enduring rite of passage.

Red Asphalt—the title says it all—is the flip side of California's carefree car culture. Intended to scare the bejabbers out of fresh-faced and obliviously immortal teen drivers, the original film and its four remakes are horror shows of vehicular ultraviolence mostly filmed by camera-ready cops called to accident scenes along the state's roads. The gruesome road-splatter films have become sociological touchstones for many drivers and even may be among the most-viewed movie titles ever to come out of California.

"What you're about to see is not going to entertain you," warns the host of *Red Asphalt III*, whose no-nonsense introduction is typical of the films in the series. "There are scenes of human suffering and death in stark reality. We did not enjoy making this film, and we don't expect you to enjoy watching it."

Thus welcomed, you're off on a joyless ride of grim highway fatality statistics, hectoring commentary about driving safely, and bona fide hurl-your-cookies gore. I've just spent the better part of a week watching all of them, one after another, and came away with three unforgettable impressions:

- Driving at more than 10 mph is a seriously bad idea.
- Anyone who ever lobbied against seat belts and air bags as standard equipment should be arrested, tried, and executed, ideally all in the same day.
- Not even George Romero has come close to replicating the sight and sound of human viscera being hand-scooped off damp pavement and into a plastic bag.

Perhaps it's hard to believe that this kind of "shockumentary" was not a California invention. That honor goes to Ohio, which in 1959 released *Signal 30*, a no-budget sixteen-millimeter movie that features some of the worst acting ever committed to celluloid, comically wooden dialogue, and a musical soundtrack so melodramatic that Boris Karloff really should have had the starring role. Without it or its spawn—*Mechanized Death* and *Wheels of Tragedy*—*Red Asphalt* might never have been filmed.

"Frankly, we were trying to give California its own version of the Ohio film," recalls seventy-eight-year-old Kent Milton, who was doing media relations for the CHP in the early 1960s when work began on the original *Red Asphalt*. "We wanted our own brand name on it to help promote the CHP."

Tastes change, of course, and to remain real and relevant to each new generation, *Red Asphalt* has gone through a series of remakes. No matter how riveting the accident-scene footage, a mashed lead-sled from the late 1950s will have less effect on today's teens than seeing a Nissan Maxima like theirs wrapped around a tree. Plus, the CHP has learned a few cinematic tricks from Hollywood over the years. Early examples of the genre were screechy, preachy variations of the now-kitschy *Reefer Madness* governmental scare flick. *Signal 30*, for instance, opens with the sounds of a crash, followed by a text crawl that belongs in the Museum of Turgid Prose:

"This is not a Hollywood movie as can be readily seen. The quality is below their standards. However . . . nothing has been staged. These are actual scenes taken immediately after the accidents occurred. Also, unlike Hollywood, our actors are paid nothing. Most of the actors in these movies are bad actors and received top billing only on a tombstone. They paid a terrific price to be in these movies, they paid with their lives."

Back then, the images were just as unsophisticated as the narration. Accident-scene footage showed harshly lighted people standing around gawking at all forms of debris as if watching a peep show. Later versions incorporated scenes of rescue efforts to save the movies' unfortunate stars, reflecting the evolution of emergency techniques and equipment.

The melodramatic title sequence from the *Red Asphalt V* DVD
PHOTOGRAPH BY MARTIN J. SMITH FROM A DVD SUPPLIED BY DOUG WEST OF THE CALIFORNIA HIGHWAY PATROL

By *Red Asphalt III*, the CHP was interspersing carnage clips with interviews featuring accident investigators and commentary from actor Scott DeVenney (who reacts with head-shaking "How do you people live with yourselves?" contempt) and a uniformed CHP officer. Unfortunately, the studio set of *Red Asphalt III* revolves around a couple of ancient, boxy Apple Macintosh computers, which now look hopelessly dated.

The fourth version, released in 1998, included interviews with victims' families and friends to add emotional power to the shock value. That version also represented a cinematic leap in terms of music, lighting, and camera work.

Red Asphalt V, the latest version that came out last year, features what a CHP spokesman called a "Matt Damon–type" actor who delivers the introduction and litany of statistics wearing layered shirts, jeans, and a reasonably cool haircut. The makers of *Asphalt V* have borrowed from cinema verité, employing audiotape of a 911 emergency call and graveside testimonials. Its opening sequence might make Brian De Palma proud: A road flare is struck and hisses to life, followed by a suspenseful nighttime tracking shot in which the beam of a flashlight plays first across roadside vegetation, then finds the first hints of automotive debris, and finally illuminates a bloody victim trapped inside the metal crumple that once was a car.

But the question remains: Do these films actually shape or change driving habits?

Maury Hannigan believes they do. Hannigan, a former CHP commissioner who oversaw production of *Asphalt III* and current vice president of public-safety solutions for ACS Inc., an international computer-services company, argues that fear is a great motivator when it comes to behavior modification. There's nothing quite like the sight of once-vital young bodies broken open or bent into improbable angles to "get the brain cells working," he says.

"When you get into an automobile, there's this sense of independence, that you're not vulnerable to the outside world, that this steel capsule is going to protect you," Hannigan says. "But people don't understand the kinetic energy that's involved in a collision at thirty, forty, fifty miles per hour."

"There's reality TV, and then there's this," agrees Tom Marshall, a spokesman for the CHP in Sacramento. "Does it make you change your driving habits forever? No. But if it can get kids to focus on it for the first month or two [that they're driving], it has done its job."

POSTSCRIPT

This essay is adapted from a story that originally appeared in the June 21, 2006, issue of the Los Angeles Times. *The* Red Asphalt *public-service film series is now available on DVD. The latest installment, 2006's* Red Asphalt V, *received an average Amazon rating of four-and-a-half stars out of five, including one from a reviewer who wrote, "I buy this every time a new edition is made. I am a therapist and owner of an addiction treatment program. Live in remote area where a victims panel is not available for DUI offenders. Red Asphalt is used in place of that. Great tool, will continue to buy this product."*

CHAPTER EIGHT

Lynne Cox's Incomparable Wake

Sunny Southern California is full of high-level athletes. Lynne Cox set herself apart by swimming three miles through water cold enough to kill most people in thirty minutes. (2012)

PLENTY OF ATHLETES ACCOMPLISHED THE EXTRAORDINARY IN 1987. Wayne Gretzky was the National Hockey League's top scorer and most valuable player, and his Edmonton Oilers also won the Stanley Cup. Martina Navratilova won Wimbledon and the US Open. And Ireland's Stephen Roche won an amazing cycling trifecta—the Giro d'Italia, the Tour de France, and the Road World Cycling Championship.

To me, though, the most significant sports accomplishment that year—by perhaps the most remarkable athlete California has ever produced—took place far from a stadium or arena, without much media coverage or any significant prizes, trophies, or endorsement deals. Twenty-five years ago, at 9:30 a.m. on August 7, Lynne Cox, a charming, gregarious, thirty-year-old open-water distance swimmer from Los Alamitos, made her way to the rocky waterline of an Alaskan island called Little Diomede, between the Bering and Chukchi Seas. Dense fog shrouded the small group of Inuit locals, journalists, doctors, and volunteers who'd gathered, waiting to see if she'd really do what she spent eleven years planning, training, and negotiating to do.

At five-foot-six, shivering in only a thin one-piece swimsuit and holding her yellow bathing cap and swim goggles, Cox couldn't see her destination, Big Diomede, but she knew the island was out there in the foreboding gray, nearly three miles across the frigid Bering Strait in what was then the Soviet Union. Equally unseen were two Soviet navy vessels, which, as promised, awaited her arrival at the international date line, the border between the world's preeminent superpowers. It had been closed to boats since 1948 and had never been swum.

Then Cox did the unthinkable. Without benefit of an insulating wet-suit or grease, and without anyone in her home country much noticing, she pulled her bathing cap over her bobbed hair, snapped her goggles into place, and stepped into water between thirty-eight and forty-four degrees—so cold that, had it been about ten degrees cooler, she could have skated across.

Surely you can imagine the pain.

Our most familiar athletes are the ones with the big contracts and unfathomable endorsement deals, or those whose boorish behavior or criminal records make them famous for entirely different reasons. That's not to diminish the achievements of our thoroughbreds. Watch the silky glide of Kobe Bryant through traffic in the paint or the raw power of Misty May-Treanor rocketing from the sand to spike a volleyball and you know immediately that, yes, they're different from you and me. I don't begrudge them their medals, trophies, fame, and wealth. They've worked hard for everything they've achieved.

But I'm writing this homage to Lynne Cox on the twenty-fifth anni-versary of her Bering Strait swim because our culture sometimes over-looks those who accomplish remarkable feats and still remain admirably grounded, who have no hope of widespread public acclaim, who never convert their accomplishments into significant cash.

The short version of Cox's story is that she recognized her almost singular talent as an open-water marathon swimmer at an early age and then worked like a demon to develop it. She's not exceptionally fast in a pool, but her endurance and will in the unpredictable, open ocean are astounding. At fourteen, she swam the twenty-seven-mile Santa Catalina Channel. A year later, in 1972, she broke the men's and women's records for the nearly twenty-four-mile English Channel swim between the UK and France, completing the legendary crossing in nine hours and

Lynne Cox's endurance and will in the open ocean are legendary.
PHOTO BY MICHAEL MULLER/CPI SYNDICATION, AND USED WITH PERMISSION

fifty-seven minutes. Someone else broke her record not long after, so she returned in 1973 and improved her time to nine hours and thirty-six minutes, again breaking the men's record. Those feats alone might have been enough to get her inducted into the Swimming Hall of Fame, and in 2000, she was.

But for young Cox, early success brought about a sort of existential crisis: "After you've broken a world record twice, why go back again? What more can you do with it?"

Cox found her true calling at age eighteen in the middle of a grueling 1975 swim across the eleven-mile Cook Strait between New Zealand's north and south islands, the first by a woman. As she struggled for more than twelve hours against high waves and currents that stretched the distance to twenty-one miles, her crew began to tell her about the supportive calls flowing into Radio Wellington, which was covering the swim live. One came from the country's prime minister. At one point, the captain of a cross-channel ferry risked his job by abandoning his regular route to get closer to Cox. He urged his four hundred passengers outside to cheer her on, and raised an American flag in tribute to her efforts.

"That's when I realized a swim could be a powerful thing," Cox recalls.

Thus began a lifelong odyssey. Instead of trying to break records, she began a series of swims that were the first of their kind or staged in locations that presented an opportunity to shine a spotlight where political tensions ran high. It took her more than a decade of complicated negotiations to pull off the 1987 Bering Strait swim, which later was toasted at the White House by President Reagan and visiting Soviet President Mikhail Gorbachev as a landmark in thawing US–Soviet relations. The following year, I tagged along as a newspaper reporter to chronicle her swim across Siberia's Lake Baikal, the world's oldest and deepest lake, against the backdrop of a crumbling Soviet bloc. There, in that remote region of the planet, I saw thousands of Soviet citizens greet her as a hero as she climbed out of the water.

In 1990, the year after the Berlin Wall fell, reuniting the German nations, she swam the Spree River from East to West Berlin, passing white crosses that marked where more desperate swimmers had been shot dead along that once-tense border. In 1994, she swam through the Gulf of Aqaba from Egypt to Israel, and then from Israel to Jordan.

Still, she remained mostly unknown, even in Orange County, where she often trains by swimming between jetties near the Seal Beach Pier.

By then, Cox already was offering herself to another cause—medical research. Scientists had long marveled at her ability to survive water temperatures that would kill most people. Could the lessons learned from studying Cox provide medical insights? She willingly became a guinea pig, submitting herself to rigorous testing. For the Bering Strait swim, she swallowed an uncomfortably large thermo-sensitive metal capsule that transmitted her body's core temperature to researchers, then politely returned the expensive device the next day in a plastic bag. She also managed that swim while enduring a cumbersome rectal probe. A University of London researcher once had her spend hours in a tank of forty-two-degree water and also submerged her hand in thirty-two-degree water for half an hour. ("One of the most painful things I've ever done in my life.") She did it all with unwavering good humor and sincere curiosity about what makes her different.

In 2002, at the age of forty-five, determined to push herself to the extreme, she plunged into thirty-two-degree water about a mile from the Antarctic ice shelf and swam more than a mile to shore, steering around sharp-edged ice floes, escorted by curious penguins. By then, the seemingly impossible things she was doing were getting hard to ignore, so CBS's *60 Minutes* sent a film crew and correspondent Scott Pelley along to witness what otherwise might have been unbelievable.

What's really unbelievable, to me, is that at a time when twenty-four-hour sports programming creates borderline idolatry, Cox went a different direction—her own. Television networks work hard during the Olympics to mint a new generation of sports heroes hoping to cash in. But think about the current crop of elites: golf's Tiger Woods and Phil Mickelson; basketball's Bryant and LeBron James; soccer's David Beckham, Abby Wambach, and Lionel Messi; baseball's Albert Pujols, Mariano Rivera, and Alex Rodriguez; tennis's Roger Federer; auto racing's Michael Schumacher; and surfing's Kelly Slater. Every one is an athletic treasure. But other than sheer excellence in their sport and the occasional charitable foundation, what do they stand for? Gatorade? Nike? Adidas? Pfizer? Samsung?

Only the rarest athletes become bigger than their sport and themselves. Seats at that table are reserved for cultural symbols: Jesse Owens, Jackie Robinson, Muhammad Ali, Billie Jean King. You know *their* names because they excelled in competitive sports played out in dramatic fashion before massive audiences and in most cases also reaped commercial rewards. You don't know much about Cox because she pursued greatness far from the spotlight, and often at the ends of the Earth.

In a 1999 profile of her in the *New Yorker*, Charles Sprawson summed up the essential truth about this one-of-a-kind swimmer: "Cox's life has been a form of knightly quest, and her spirit has remained essentially romantic."

When it came time to tell her own story, Cox did so with similarly inspiring results. She had been trying for years to write a memoir about her extraordinary life. After her Antarctic adventure became the capstone to her swimming career, she focused on a new challenge: to conquer the unpredictable waters of publishing. She proved no less determined to succeed than during her channel-swimming days, and she sometimes struggled just as hard. But she persisted. And, of course, succeeded.

When her 2005 memoir, *Swimming to Antarctica*, was published, it hit the *New York Times* bestseller list. A year later, her second book, *Grayson*, a lyrical account of her encounter with a lost baby gray whale during a training swim off Seal Beach, also landed on that coveted list and later was translated into sixteen languages. She wrote a 2008 story for the *New Yorker* about swimming portions of the Northwest Passage from Greenland to Alaska—using Roald Amundsen's account of his journey as her guide—and it presaged her third book, *South with the Sun: Roald Amundsen, His Polar Explorations, and the Quest for Discovery*, published in 2011.

Cox has pursued her writing with unwavering commitment and the same steely will that has propelled her across some of the world's most dangerous waters. And that's why, decades after I first met her, she remains an inspiration—not because she's an elite athlete, but because she embodies two fundamental truths: It's possible to succeed spectacularly by just being yourself, and true greatness requires you to be bigger than that.

POSTSCRIPT

This article is adapted from one that originally appeared in the August 2012 issue of Orange Coast *magazine. Cox continues to swim and write, and often delivers motivational speeches. She is the author of six books: the auto-biographical* Swimming to Antarctica *and* Grayson, *as well as* South with the Sun; Open Water Swimming Manual; Elizabeth, Queen of the Seas; *and* Swimming in the Sink.

CHAPTER NINE

Lamenting Liberace

Talking celebrity, legacy, and mortality with the faithful outside the dying entertainer's Palm Springs home (1987)

THE GREAT MAN ONCE STEAMROLLED PETITE HELEN MUSENGO AT the Hacienda Casino in Las Vegas. It was a special moment for her, so when she heard the flamboyant entertainer was dying, she naturally wanted to join dozens of other fans keeping a deathwatch outside Liberace's Palm Springs home.

"I feel close to him," she says, waiting with her pocket camera across the street from the front door through which many believe the pianist's body eventually will be brought. "I was playing a one-armed bandit and Liberace came in to watch a dinner show. He parked his Rolls-Royce in the back and was walking through the casino and he just knocked me down!"

"Do you know who just knocked you down?" her husband, Mike, had asked that enchanted evening so long ago. She'd caught a glimpse of a sweeping, floor-length mink coat but hadn't noticed the face of the man who, she said, just kept walking.

Musengo remembers being picked up and dusted off by two burly bodyguards, but she didn't realize she'd had a brush with stardom until her husband filled her in. "I went around telling people that Liberace knocked me down," the sixty-seven-year-old Fort Lauderdale, Florida, resident says. An apology would have been nice, she adds, "because then I could have said I talked to him."

Everybody outside Casa de Liberace on Wednesday has their own special reason for being near the entertainer during his final hours. While Liberace struggles inside the Spanish-style home with what his manager said is pernicious anemia, advanced emphysema, and heart disease, the vigil-keepers carry out their social duty. They hang over a low block wall across the street from the home, a constant murmur of speculation and ever-changing parade of pastel jogging suits, Spandex pants, and gold jewelry. They swap memories with other fans and enthusiastically reminisce for the action-starved reporters and photographers.

"I didn't want to come around here like a vulture, but what the hell," says sixty-five-year-old Marcel Tallieu, of Winnipeg, Canada. "I just wanted to see his house once more."

He is hardly alone. Tour vans and charter buses meander along Belardo Road between the casa and the crowds. Minicams stare unblinkingly from their tripods waiting to record the inevitable and apparently imminent. The crowd is generally well behaved except for one man arrested by Palm Springs police for trying to steal a purse from a spectator's pickup truck. At one point, hours before Liberace dies, a paparazzo in a rented helicopter hovers over the house under the mistaken impression that a hearse is set to remove the entertainer's body. Eventually the helicopter disappears, and the tedious wait resumes.

Herbert and Genevieve House of St. Louis recruit an idle news photographer to shoot their portrait outside the home where Liberace lay dying. They stand on the curb in front of the showman's trampled petunia bed, join arms, and smile.

Click.

"We've been married fifty-four years," Genevieve says. "We've got ten grandkids, and one great-grand, and they always want to know if we saw any movie stars while we were in Palm Springs." The picture is for them, she says.

The most dedicated of those gathered is George Finney of Arkansas, whose mission today speaks to our peculiar fascination with those in the celebrity spotlight. Finney says he trailed Liberace for months in his battered 1974 Dodge Monaco trying to get an autographed picture. "Everywhere he went in the United States, I was there," Finney says. "Las

Liberace's grave at Forest Lawn Hollywood Hills in Los Angeles, California.
[CC BY-SA 3.0 (HTTP://CREATIVECOMMONS.ORG/LICENSES/BY-SA/3.0) OR GFDL (HTTP://WWW
.GNU.ORG/COPYLEFT/FDL.HTML)], FROM WIKIMEDIA COMMONS

Vegas, Denver, New Jersey. I slept in lobbies where he's appeared and I've been living in my car the last couple of months, but the man doesn't even know I'm alive."

Perched with his binoculars on the Monaco's hood, he draws deeply on an unfiltered cigarette. "I'm not out here to gawk at him. I sold everything I had just so I could give him this flag off my daddy's grave and get a picture to bury with my dad."

The forty-one-year-old Finney says his father, a devoted Liberace fan, died eight years ago and is buried in Gary, Indiana, along with two boxes of the star's albums. The picture is something Finney is sure his father would want as well, but his attempts to get one have been frustrated. The task has proved especially difficult for Finney because he is not a Liberace fan.

"But I won't give up," he says. "All I want is an autographed picture or a signed statement that I'll get one in the mail, and I'll be out of the man's hair."

John "Kid" Hoppe wanders by about 2 p.m. "I'd like to buy [Liberace's] house," says the eighty-one-year-old Hoppe. "I want it for my kids because I like the white orchid tree near the front door. But I don't want to do anything until everything is . . ." He pauses. "Settled. You never know. He may live."

But Liberace's body is brought out the front door of his home about 3:20 p.m., and the crowd begins thinning out. Finney had displayed his father's flag jutting from the Monaco's window since his arrival more than a week before and rolls it carefully onto its pole. He finally gets some closure when Liberace's manager later accepts the flag, and Finney leaves with a promise that an autographed picture will soon be on its way.

"I'm ashamed I drove out here, because they said it was a circus," Finney says. "They talk about us being rude and telling us we don't have the right to be here. But we made this man what he is today, and I've got every right to be here. My spot's paid for."

POSTSCRIPT

This story is adapted from one that appeared in the Orange County Register *on February 5, 1987, the day after Liberace's death. It's hard to say how, or if, subsequent revelations that the entertainer died from complications of AIDS or allegations that he'd infected some of his unwitting lovers with the then-deadly HIV affected those who were there that day. But the moment did create a watermark in the history of the disease. If the 1980s were all about secrecy, mystery, Rock Hudson, and snickering White House news conferences dismissing questions about the "gay plague," the decade that followed was characterized by awareness, openness, and Los Angeles Lakers superstar Ervin "Magic" Johnson, whose announcement on November 7, 1991, that he was infected was a milestone in public awareness and acceptance.*

CHAPTER TEN

The Birdman of Mojave

Taking risks and breaking rules with Voyager *creator Burt Rutan, whose creative high-desert hijinks revolutionized modern aircraft design (1986 and 1987)*

UNTIL HE WAS ABOUT TEN, ELBERT "BURT" RUTAN LIVED THE KID brother's fate. He often watched from the sidelines as his irrepressible older brother, Dick, built and flew his model airplanes. To parents George and Irene Rutan, in fact, Burt seemed strangely content to fish his brother's mangled models out of the wastebasket and experiment with the pieces. By the time Irene took him to a hobby shop near their home near Fresno looking for a simple beginner's kit, he balked.

"Burt didn't want that," says his father, now living in Palmdale. "He wanted a sheet of white paper. So Irene took him to the butcher shop and got him some paper, and he came home and sketched it out. It was a skeleton framework deal. He built this thing with a four- or five-foot wingspan out of rice paper and little pieces of balsa. From then on, I don't think he ever bought a kit."

In the decades since that first design, Burt Rutan has continued to do things his way. First as a competitive model builder, then as a designer of homebuilt recreational airplanes, now as head of Scaled Composites Inc., the research aircraft company he founded in 1982 in Mojave, California, a lonely high-desert magnet for aviation wonks. Rutan has trampled convention time and again with his unorthodox but aerodynamically ingenious airplanes.

The most famous member of his menagerie is *Voyager*, the almost ethereal airplane that one year ago today began its triumphant nine-day, twenty-five-thousand-mile nonstop flight around the world without refueling. *Voyager* grabbed Americans' imaginations in a year that opened with NASA's *Challenger* disaster, and the fascination continues. A *National Geographic* special about the project recently aired, the book is written and released, and the *Voyager* exhibit will be unveiled later today at the National Air and Space Museum in Washington, DC.

But continuing publicity about that project overshadows an almost equally astonishing accomplishment. Before the end of this month, the Rutan-inspired Starship 1 will be certified by the Federal Aviation Administration and will become the centerpiece of Beech Aircraft Corp.'s business airplane fleet. "Starship represents the greatest leap in aviation technology in a long time," says Beech spokesman Drew Steketee at company headquarters in Wichita, Kansas. "There's never been anything like it. Ever."

Long considered too radical for the general aviation industry, Rutan's ideas are now being embraced by aviation's mainstream. (Think of him each time you notice the upturned "winglets" at the end of the wing on

Burt Rutan on the flight line at Mojave (California) Airport, March 2011
AL SEIB © 2011, *LOS ANGELES TIMES.* USED WITH PERMISSION.

your next commercial flight.) His work with Beechcraft is as though New Ager Shirley MacLaine was suddenly given a cabinet post. Rutan now is being called "visionary" by aviation-industry insiders for his work with lightweight composite airframes. He often is compared to aviation pioneers such as John Northrup and Donald Douglas. And his son, Jeffrey, unabashedly calls his father "a modern-day Leonardo da Vinci."

At the center of that heady praise is a gangly, likeable forty-four-year-old who in some ways still acts like the kid who transformed wrecked models. After years of tinkering with aviation dogma in this high-desert town, he's anxious to share his success with a nation he feels no longer is willing to challenge the odds. "The lesson of *Voyager* is this," says the Birdman of Mojave. "You can't sit fat, dumb, and happy and do only conservative things."

Risk has a shape, and one recent afternoon it was sitting along the Mojave Airport flight line. It was the latest prototype airplane to emerge from the Scaled Composites hangar.

Like most of its predecessors, the stubby white aircraft seemed to break a lot of aerodynamic rules. But unlike some of Rutan's earlier designs, which by conventional measure seemed to fly backward or maybe upside-down, this one simply looked as if it had too many wings. As Rutan paced around his creation, in his characteristic headlong stride, the awkward, arguably eccentric plane seemed an appropriate reflection of its creator, whom friends and colleagues often describe with some variation of the phrase "Burt is Burt."

It's an understandable dodge. In many ways, Rutan is a walking anomaly, a man who throughout the upscale, dress-for-success 1980s has clung to his muttonchop sideburns, open collars, and cowboy boots. How should one describe a man who keeps a Styrofoam pterodactyl skeleton suspended from his living room ceiling, and who since parting with his third wife has shared his Palmdale home with Starship and Winglet, a brooding hyacinthine macaw and a talkative African gray parrot?

"He's just Burt," says Bruce Evans, who served as crew chief on the *Voyager* project. "He doesn't make a point about trying to be unconventional. That's just the way he is. He doesn't make a point of his unusual airplane designs, either. That's just the way he thinks they should be."

Rutan is the man who, during a postflight news conference shortly after *Voyager*'s triumphant landing December 23, 1986, slipped away from the clamoring media to answer his nagging question about bug guts. While his brother and Jeana Yeager—who built and copiloted *Voyager*—were being hailed as the nation's newest aviation heroes, Rutan was counting "insect strikes" along *Voyager*'s main wing. Bug guts cause drag, and drag burns fuel. In an equation filled with so many variables, the consummate engineer was anxious to fill in some *X*s. (A year later, he remembered the count: sixty-eight bugs.)

Rutan is bored easily, and his eyes often wander during conversation. "The whole time you're with him, he's designing or naming or flying some airplane," his mother says. "If you don't tune into airplanes, then he's not even hearing you."

Rutan, a Beech vice president since the aircraft giant bought Scaled Composites in 1985, wears a suit when necessary, although often with boots. During public speaking engagements he makes little effort to tone down his dry, occasionally naughty sense of humor. "Burt is Burt," says Dan Card, a Yosemite National Park manager who worked as volunteer general manager on the *Voyager* project. "He's himself wherever he is. I think it's a family trait. They [Burt and Dick] don't pay attention to social norms. It's not a lack of social graces, don't get me wrong, but they just don't care. You either accept them, or you don't.

"That's their philosophy," Card says. "They say, 'We're going to do this our way.' And that has allowed Burt to make some great strides in aviation. He's not constrained by all the norms, and he's been able to translate that quirk of his personality into engineering terms."

The roots of that philosophy reach back to the early 1960s, when Rutan was studying aeronautical engineering at California Polytechnic University. Burt was "too busy doing his own thing" to develop childhood heroes, says his father, but that apparently changed when word began to spread about a new airplane—Lockheed's super-secret SR-71.

Twenty-four years after its introduction, the SR-71—a sleek, titanium-alloy reconnaissance jet capable of flying more than three times the speed of sound—still is regarded as the world's fastest airplane.

According to *Jane's All the World's Aircraft*, the SR-71, nicknamed "Black-bird," "remains unrivaled in terms of sheer performance."

Rutan's eyes still brighten when he talks about it. "When it was first revealed in 1964, it was the most significant advance of any airplane ever," he says. When asked in November about his role models, the first name Rutan mentioned was that of Kelly Johnson, who headed the research team that developed the SR-71. But as much as Rutan admires the technological leap the SR-71 represents, he says he also learned a lot from Johnson's methods.

"Kelly Johnson's most important rule is this," he says. "When you're doing pure research, it has to be done in an environment with as few people and organizations involved as is absolutely possible."

Rutan adopted that rule in the mid-1970s after he began designing a series of homebuilt airplanes, the plans for which he sold to thousands of recreational aviation enthusiasts. In addition to using lightweight composite materials and pusher engines, many Rutan designs include canards, small forward wings that provide added lift and help keep the planes from stalling. It's an idea that goes back to the Wright brothers, but one Rutan salvaged from aviation's wastebasket and recast into his trademark.

Rutan's creative abilities sometimes leave his daughter-in-law "spell-bound." Jessica Rutan, a teacher at Woodbury Elementary School in Garden Grove, California, says Rutan and her husband, Jeff, share an approach to problem solving that transcends the fact that one designs airplanes and the other designs computer software with Hughes Air-craft. "They're always looking for something new," she says. "They think, 'There's got to be a better way, a faster way of doing this. This plane can do something better.'"

Like Rutan's airplanes, Scaled Composites reflects its creator. "You should see the staff meetings up there," says sixty-nine-year-old Fergus Fay of La Mirada, who worked as a volunteer flight mechanic on the *Voyager* project. "They would make the Rockwell people turn pale. There's people in jeans and sports shirts lying around on the floor, people drinking coffee, laughing, making remarks."

But Scaled has proved itself a workable vehicle for Rutan's creativity. Although the company now is a subsidiary of Beech, Rutan also works on independent contracts. The arrangement allows him to design airplanes, build prototypes, and flight-test his ideas without the relative drudgery of actually producing and selling them. While the manufacturer who contracts one of his planes must struggle with production problems and FAA certification, Rutan is happily onto the next design.

"We take care to recognize Burt Rutan's genius and not smother it," Beech's Steketee says of their arm's-length relationship. "He is purposefully apart to allow him the opportunity to pursue his creativity and test fresh ideas, but he does have responsibilities to address the practical and the budgetary. Of course, the two worlds have to do battle."

Even when they do, Rutan sometimes gets his way. Rutan says he currently is designing a military airplane, which he offered to build and flight-test for a bargain price. He insisted, though, that government auditors not hang around his shop. After finding out what the same work would cost elsewhere, the government finally gave Scaled the contract, and on Rutan's terms. When he talks about it, he does so with the confident air of a victor.

When he's frustrated, though, Rutan talks passionately about how America is grinding to a creative halt—in general aviation, the auto industry, and space exploration, among other things—because second-guessing MBAs and product-liability lawyers have taken over where engineers once flourished. During a question-and-answer period after a recent speech, someone asked Rutan if they could still buy plans for one of his popular homebuilt airplanes. His answer was surprisingly bitter.

"I stopped selling them two-and-a-half years ago," he said. "Lawyers have a philosophy in this country that people shouldn't be allowed to take risks. You watch that. If someone tells you they have a proposition for you without any risks, watch out that he's not trying to take away your freedom."

Such talk might seem heresy in the general aviation industry, which has seen aircraft sales drop from an estimated eighteen thousand in 1979 to only one thousand this year. But about the time that slump began to worsen, Beech began planning its next generation of airplanes.

The company wanted to build an eight- to ten-seat propeller plane, and three of the thirteen designs submitted were so heavily influenced by Rutan's work in the 1970s that Beech asked Rutan to serve as a design consultant and to build the prototype. Eventually, Beech bought Rutan's little desert company and made Rutan a Beech vice president. He still remains president and chief executive officer of his firm.

The result is Starship 1, a predominantly composite airplane whose distinctive silhouette now graces the front cover of Beech's business airplane catalog. Rutan's impact is apparent in Starship's pusher engines, upturned wingtips, and small forward wings. "Beechcraft," the motto beneath the photograph reads, "where new ideas take flight."

When *Voyager* is unveiled today at the National Air and Space Museum, the general public will see it among birds of a similar feather—the 1903 *Wright Flyer*, Charles Lindbergh's *Spirit of St. Louis*, the Bell X-1, and the North American X-15.

There's not a safe plane among them.

Voyager, for example, was a massive risk from the start, a plan to more than double the existing 12,532-mile record for nonstop, nonrefueled flight by a US Air Force B-52. The plane was nothing more than "a drawing on a piece of paper and three kooks out in the desert," says Dick Rutan of his brother and Yeager, his then-girlfriend and copilot. Built without any government financing or involvement, its $544,000 cost was financed through the sale of T-shirts, caps, and other memorabilia. Its builders engaged in a high-stakes scavenger hunt for expensive equipment that drew dozens of individuals and corporations into a unique partnership. When it took off, it had no lightning protection, and its rudder pedals were "weak" and difficult to manipulate because, in an effort to save weight, Rutan had modified them significantly. Instead of a microelectronic system for managing the plane's seventeen separate fuel tanks, Rutan devised a system in which the most critical component was a large, reliable rubber band. Beyond that, he said, "most of the experts in the field felt I was stretching the equations."

Even Dick Rutan, who had test flown a number of Rutan's earlier designs, was skeptical when his brother first proposed the idea for a nonstop around-the-world flight in late 1980, and then sketched an unusual design on a napkin at the old Mojave Inn. "This is the same guy who thinks we can build a human-powered vehicle and pedal it into Earth orbit," Dick says. "The poor guy has so many airplane designs running around in his head he just can't get them all out. I don't know what his genius is—he's not telling anybody—but he sets it all down on paper and it's always very close."

For example, when *Voyager* was still just a piece of paper, Burt estimated that without engines or equipment, the plane's structure would weigh 935.5 pounds. Although the acceptable margin of error on that weight calculation was approximately ninety-three pounds, he was off by only three-and-a-half.

Burt envisioned *Voyager* as a creature of finesse, not speed or brute power. To be built almost entirely from lightweight composites, *Voyager* would weigh only 2,200 pounds when loaded with pilots, equipment, and supplies for its world flight—less than a small car. Its fragile shell, though, would contain seventeen separate tanks capable of carrying nearly five times its weight in fuel. Once those tanks were filled, he calculated, the plane would weigh 11,326 pounds.

To provide enough lift to get the fully loaded *Voyager* off the ground, the design called for a wingspan of 111 feet, about the same as a Boeing 727. To survive rough air, the main wing would have to be capable of flexing thirty feet up or down—a sixty-foot total arc—without rupturing the fuel tanks inside them. For added safety and an added sense of history during the world flight takeoff, *Voyager* would use the fifteen-thousand-foot runway at Edwards Air Force Base over which famed test pilot Chuck Yeager (no relation to Jeana) first shattered the sound barrier.

As with virtually all of Burt Rutan's designs, *Voyager* would have canards forward of the main wing. Much of the fuel would be carried in two thirty-foot outrigger booms that would sit alongside the cigar-shaped fuselage. The plane would be powered by two propeller engines—a pusher at one end, and a puller at the other, which could be turned off as the plane burned fuel and got lighter. In flight, *Voyager* would look like an enormous, sluggish dragonfly, and it would have only one practical application.

But there *Voyager* hangs, a monument to risk, the airplane that conquered the last major milestone in atmospheric flight. Challengers are inevitable, and to those who aspire to fly farther, faster, and more efficiently, Rutan offers this bit of advice:

"Break some rules, just like we did."

POSTSCRIPT

This essay is adapted from stories published September 14, 1986, and December 14, 1987, in the Orange County Register. *The* Voyager *aircraft now resides in the Smithsonian's National Air and Space Museum in Washington, DC, but that was hardly the peak accomplishment of Rutan's career. In June 2004, his* SpaceShipOne *became the first privately built and funded manned craft to reach space. Four months later, Rutan and his team won the ten-million-dollar Ansari X Prize for becoming the first nongovernment organization to launch a reusable manned spacecraft into space twice within two weeks, and then won the Collier Trophy from the National Aeronautic Association for "greatest achievement in aeronautics or astronautics in America." But a 2007 explosion in Mojave killed three engineers testing components for the next-generation* SpaceShipTwo, *and in 2010 Scale Composites announced Rutan's plan to retire in April 2011. He now lives in Couer d'Alene, Idaho. There, in 2016, he was said to be tinkering with ideas about flying cars and amphibious aircraft.*

CHAPTER ELEVEN

Honeymooning at Warp Speed

An exhausting forty-eight-hour tour of the American dream factory with Japanese couples experiencing America mostly through a bus window (1989)

THE IDEA OF SPENDING THREE HOURS ON A TRAIN AND NINE-AND-A-half hours on a plane for a six-hour bus tour of Los Angeles, a dinner aboard the anchored *Queen Mary*, and the chance to spend a day standing in Disneyland lines isn't half as astounding as the fact that, at the moment, Japanese honeymooners Akira and Hitomi Onodera are standing at all.

True, they're leaning hard against the handrail as they wait twenty minutes for the five-minute Matterhorn ride. But compared to their first two days of married life, Olympian by any measure of human endurance, the wait is a welcome break from their relentless "no options" tour of Southern California and Honolulu.

"This whole tour is just seven days from the start in Japan to the finish," explained Terry Miyahara, their Japan Travel Bureau guide, the day before as he waited for the group to clear customs at Los Angeles International Airport. "They're scheduled too tight, really, when you think about it. They're all too tired."

This, though, is the package for those who don't speak the language and don't know the customs, but who are willing to dedicate forty-eight hours to tour Los Angeles and Orange County, one of the most sprawling and diverse patches of real estate on the planet. For about two thousand dollars per person, the honeymooners can photographically validate

Tourists on the Hollywood Walk of Fame—a perennial favorite stop among Japanese honeymoon tour companies—in 2011

their presence at many local landmarks, see many other famous and not-so-famous attractions whiz past their bus window, and briefly experience the Southern California lifestyle, or at least the version of it offered in the incessant, information-packed banter of their guide.

It's an impressionistic view, for sure, but it's also the most common view given to touring Japanese. Although more leisurely tours are available, rigorous corporate and industrial work schedules in Japan—as well as a strong personal work ethic—permit only limited vacation time for most of the estimated seven hundred thousand Japanese who visited Southern California last year.

"Some of the younger Japanese are breaking away from those very structured tours, but they're still very popular," says Elaine Cali, communications director for the Anaheim Area Visitor and Convention Bureau. "They like to see a lot of things. It's a different [honeymooning] concept than most Americans are used to."

This, then, is Southern California on the fly, a view forged not so much by cultural exchange as by which side of the bus you happen to sit. Hold tight, for as our tour bus driver Mario Marroguin informs before leaving the airport, "It's showtime!"

First, a brief and insignificant word about baggage. Although the thirty-four touring honeymooners are dressed eclectically—a casual Eastern-college weekend sort of look—their luggage is startling in its uniformity. Of the twenty-nine bags stowed in the bus's belly, only two are not sturdy plastic, rollable suitcases fastened around the middle by a thick nylon strap.

Thirty minutes after the group clears customs, their restroom-equipped bus is turning left onto California Highway 1 headed for nearby Marina del Rey. Tour guide Miyahara already has loosened his tie, introduced the driver to polite applause, and begun a fast, free-form monologue about the area, which will continue almost uninterrupted until the honeymooners are shown to their Anaheim Hilton rooms about twelve hours later.

A billboard for Kirin beer along Lincoln Boulevard passes unmentioned. Then one for Sapporo beer. There's an inescapable sense that this is neither the first nor the last Japanese tour group to travel this particular route, a notion reinforced when the bus rolls to a stop in front of a koi pond in the marina's Fisherman's Village. A Dollar Express Oriental Food cafeteria is just steps away, and the place is teeming with Japanese honeymooners.

Before disembarking for their first and longest stop of the day—forty minutes—the group is given a quick lesson in American commerce. In Japanese, Miyahara explains the respective values of American coins, the need to specify a large, medium, or small soft drink, and instructs them how to respond when the scooper at the ice cream stand asks them, "One scoop or two?"

"In Japan, they're not used to having different sizes," Miyahara says later. "They just say 'Ice cream' or 'Coke.'"

The various touring groups take turns posing for group pictures arranged by the travel bureau's waiting photographer. The same tourists on other buses will turn up throughout the day at different locations, and it strikes me that a Japanese tourist could pass through Southern California on one of these trips without encountering an American who was not somehow connected with a Japanese tour.

Twelve minutes after leaving that stop, as the bus roars along Pacific Avenue just a block from unseen Venice Beach, twenty-six-year-old Hitomi Onodera, who works for an insurance company, is asleep against the shoulder of her new husband, a twenty-nine-year-old beauty supplies dealer. She awakens as the bus stops on a bluff overlooking the beach in Santa Monica.

Their guide announces: "There will be ten minutes of stretch time here."

As the couples stroll, briefly, along the oceanfront walkway and take turns photographing one another, Miyahara notes the importance of natural beauty to tourists from the congested Tokyo area. But unless you count Disneyland, where the following day the honeymooners will see artificial reefs and countless wire-guided fish, this will be as close to nature as they will get while in the continental United States.

Several brides are asleep again as the bus moves along Pico Boulevard, past Twentieth Century Fox Film Corp., and into Century City, where those still awake have the chance to photograph a parked Rolls-Royce while the bus idles at a signal. They roll toward fabled Beverly Hills for their one-block ride along Rodeo Drive. Eight minutes after entering that famous municipality, they leave the city limits and start a thirteen-minute ride along Hollywood's Sunset Strip.

They get twenty minutes at Mann's Chinese Theater to survey the foot- and handprints of film stars. (For the record—and this may be as reasonable a gauge of the American image abroad as any—the concrete squares specifically noted by the guide are those dedicated to Michael Jackson, Mickey Mouse, Elizabeth Taylor, Eddie Murphy, Marilyn Monroe, Sophia Loren, and Sylvester Stallone.)

"We usually get here around four o'clock," says Miyahara, obviously pleased that the tour arrived two hours ahead of schedule. "It's unbelievable. No traffic. Customs was smooth. The plane was early. Things are going very, very well."

Had things been going less well—and the bounce in Miyahara's step indicates that this is the exception rather than the rule—at least some of the group's forty-eight hours on the United States mainland might well have been spent in traffic jams. As the bus moves off toward the empty Hollywood Bowl—twenty minutes—Miyahara begins hawking copies of the group picture taken earlier at Marina del Rey. His sales tool is an eight-by-ten glossy of a different honeymoon group, although the setting and tired smiles are identical.

Luckily, on their way to the day tour's final stop in Little Tokyo, traffic snarls along the Hollywood Freeway. Several honeymooners are able to grab quick snapshots of the Hollywood sign as it blinks at them through gaps between the buildings and billboards.

Shortly after 3 p.m., the bus disgorges into a gift shop in Little Tokyo, a Japanese section of downtown Los Angeles, for what obviously is a high point of the day. Gift buying is a primary function for touring Japanese for two reasons. First, products generally are far less expensive in the United States than in Japan. A stuffed Mickey Mouse doll costing forty dollars here, for example, might cost two hundred dollars back home, Miyahara says. Second, Japanese tourists come from a culture where gift-giving is customary among traveling relatives.

For these and other reasons, Japanese tourists spent an estimated two billion dollars in the United States last year—more than any other visiting nationality—and American businesses clearly appreciate their patronage. At South Coast Plaza, for example, marketers at the super-high-end destination retail complex in Orange County have been courting Japanese tour operators and advertising in Japanese travel magazines. Some stores there also have begun recruiting Japanese-speaking sales clerks.

The honeymooners move through a cluster of Little Tokyo stores like locusts. After a forty-minute flurry of traveler's check-writing, they reboard their bus clutching bags of golf balls, designer belts, and voluminous ten-dollar tote bags that Miyahara pointed out in advance would be invaluable in hauling their gifts back home.

After skirting the edge of Skid Row—an aspect of the tour Miyahara says balances the opulence of Marina del Rey and Beverly Hills—the honeymooners are hauled down the Santa Ana Freeway toward the Anaheim Hilton. They're given an hour to change clothes and freshen up, then herded back onto the bus for what they were told would be a "romantic" dinner at a restaurant aboard the *Queen Mary* in Long Beach.

"We call it romantic because they can see the Long Beach waterfront view and have a nice dinner," Miyahara says as the first two busloads of honeymooners prepare to depart the Hilton for the special meal. "But there are so many couples, it's not really too romantic."

As the bus rumbles along the Garden Grove Freeway, the Onoderas are quizzed about their impressions of America. With Miyahira translating, they describe the land they had seen during the previous eight hours as "huge," "too big," and "too dangerous"—an impression they gleaned not from any unpleasant personal experiences but apparently from their guide's earlier warning about pickpockets.

Still, by ten o'clock the next morning, the Onoderas are ready for their first unguided foray into America: Disneyland! This is the unstructured part of the tour, when the couples are set adrift with only their meal coupons and maps. Even though there's a Disney theme park in Tokyo now, Miyahara says the original park in Anaheim remains a favorite among the visiting Japanese.

That much is clear as the Onoderas move slowly through the Matterhorn line. They're obviously fatigued, but they plan to see as much as possible before leaving on a flight to Honolulu at six o'clock the next morning. Although they speak little, they're smiling and awake as Akira Onodera reloads his camera.

POSTSCRIPT

This essay is adapted from a story originally published in a 1989 issue of the Orange County Register. *According to a 2013 report by the Japan America Society of Southern California, an estimated 646,000 tourists from Japan visit Southern California each year—a number boosted by the annual Anime Expo in Anaheim—and as a group they remain the top spenders among overseas visitors, with each travel party dropping $2,913. The same report notes that Southern California boasts approximately 1,800 Japanese restaurants—more than double the number located in Manhattan.*

Chapter Twelve

The Wild Duck Chase

A Southern California artist's dive deep into the strange and wonderful world of competitive duck painting (2010)

One day in November 2008, visitors to a small public park in Cypress, California, noticed a tall, athletic-looking man at the edge of a pond. His name was Mark Berger, a soft-spoken, middle-aged aerospace engineer and artist from Los Alamitos. He carried a digital camera and a sack of birdseed.

Berger was on a mission that would bring him back to Willow Park at least fifteen times that winter, always with his camera and more seed. Each time, he spent a couple of hours luring hungry American wigeon ducks within range of his viewfinder. But Berger was more than an eccentric artist communing with wild ducks; his was a deceptively ambitious pursuit. He was chasing a dream of fortune and fame down a peculiar and uniquely American rabbit hole, disappearing into a little-known wonderland of characters much like himself, a world of art, talent, ego, controversy, scandal, money, and migratory waterfowl.

Berger was preparing to enter the annual Federal Duck Stamp Contest.

If you're not a hunter or a wildlife artist or a particularly obsessive fan of iconoclastic filmmakers Joel and Ethan Coen, then you've likely never heard of this quirky bit of Americana. Even though it has been around for seventy-five years as the only juried art competition run by the federal government, and even though it has become what one recent news story called the "Academy Awards of wildlife stamp art," it certainly is well off the cultural radar.

"You'd figure that if the federal government was going to have one juried art competition, it'd come out of the National Endowment for the Arts, not Fish and Wildlife," says Patricia Fisher, chief of the Federal Duck Stamp Program. "But there we are."

So, for newcomers to this unusual and mostly overlooked tradition, a quick tutorial. We're not talking postage stamps here. That misconception was created, in part, by the Coen brothers' 1996 film *Fargo*, with its subplot in which Norm Gunderson, the husband of pregnant police chief Marge Gunderson, obsesses about his painting and its chances in that year's duck stamp contest. In an inspired bit of Coenesque dialogue at the end of the movie, Norm quietly announces how his painting fared:

Norm: They announced it.

Marge: They announced it?

Norm: Yeah.

Marge: So?

Norm: Three-cent stamp.

Marge: Your mallard?

Norm: Yeah.

Marge: Oh, that's terrific.

Norm: It's just a three-cent stamp.

Marge: It's terrific.

Norm: Hautman's blue-winged teal got the twenty-nine-cent. People don't much use the three-cent.

Marge: Oh, for Pete's sake. Of course they do. Whenever they raise the postage, people need the little stamps.

In fact, the Federal Duck Stamp is not a postage stamp but the stamp that for decades all waterfowl hunters over the age of sixteen have been required to buy and carry. This year about one and a half million hunters, conservationists, and collectors will pay fifteen dollars for the stamp,

Minnesota's Hautman brothers, including Joe in the ghillie suit, are the New York Yankees of competitive duck painting.
PHOTO BY DAVID BOWMAN, USED WITH PERMISSION

which also entitles bearers to free admission to all national wildlife refuges. Since passage of the 1934 Bird Hunting Stamp Act, ninety-eight cents of every dollar spent on each stamp has gone to the Migratory Bird Conservation Fund to buy wetlands and wildlife habitat for inclusion in the National Wildlife Refuge System, which protects those resources for future generations. The estimated $750 million raised so far has been used to preserve more than five million acres of wetland and habitat; many other countries and states, including California since 1971, have copied the program. Trumpets the US Fish and Wildlife Service brochure: "Little wonder the Federal Duck Stamp Program has been called one of the most successful conservation programs ever initiated."

All well and good, but the overarching and noble purpose of the competition doesn't really tell the story of the strange and fascinating annual drama it has created. To understand that—and this is where Berger comes in—you need to understand exactly what it means to hold the odd-but-official title of Federal Duck Stamp Artist.

When the program began, Fish and Wildlife asked selected artists to submit designs for the stamp. But starting in 1949, the government opened the competition to the public. For professional and amateur wildlife artists, the contest immediately became that rarest of things: a chance to instantly claim some measure of artistic immortality.

"I call it America's first reality show," says program chief Fisher. "*American Idol* for wildlife artists."

So once a year, about two hundred artists embark on a quest. During the contest's seventy-five years, legends have been born, dreams have died, and controversies have rocked the competition, including the year organizers realized the judges had chosen a winner that was missing key flight feathers. (The artist had used a domesticated, clipped-wing duck as his model.) The competitors' annual effort to overcome obscurity, make a fortune, and leave their mark on the world is nothing less than a pure expression of the American dream.

At fifty-five, Berger had no particular interest in painting ducks, but he found the notion of painting ducks as a *sport* compelling: "I was drawn to the contest and the idea of becoming a better painter. But I'm fairly competitive by nature and enjoy that aspect of it."

As a younger man, he learned to compete as a standout shortstop in high school and a walk-on baseball talent at Penn State, where he also studied mechanical engineering. He migrated to the aerospace mecca of Southern California and worked for companies such as Hughes, Rockwell, McDonnell Douglas, and Boeing for the past thirty-two years. His fine analytical mind and knack for detail have served him well on programs such as the space shuttle, the space station, and the upper stage of the Delta III rocket. To an aerospace engineer, the world is a numbers game, a reassuring calculus in which, if you adjust for the x factors, the outcome is predetermined. People like that find something affirming, almost holy, in the beautiful certainty of math.

As a parent, he is no less committed to his sons, Seth and Nathan, and spent years coaching in sports leagues in Los Alamitos, where he and his family have lived since 1989, and where we were neighbors for several years. But as Berger's kids grew up and as his time gradually became his own again, he decided in 2003 to take up a new hobby. He began to paint. And once a competitor, always a competitor.

As you might expect, Berger pursues his passions methodically and with an engineer's careful calculation. By May 2008, he was ready to test himself. He entered a painting of the Seal Beach strand in the Sunset Beach Art Festival, his first competition, and the piece was named best in show. In addition to that confidence booster, he also began to understand that his art might have more tangible value. The next year, for example, he was able to trade two of his paintings for a twelve-year-old Infiniti Q45 for his older son.

About that time, as Berger and wife Kathy prepared for life in an empty nest, he casually mentioned he was entering one of his paintings in an art competition that, to uninitiated souls like me, sounded patently absurd and improbable. And when he uttered one particularly unforgettable line during a recent bike ride—"You know, the Hautman brothers are like the New York Yankees of the duck stamp contest"—I had to know more. I also wondered if he knew what he was getting himself into.

Engineering and sports are very different from art, of course, and Berger was stepping into a world where the comforting and precise rules of science don't apply, where everything is subjective. Because of that, the history of the pro-am Federal Duck Stamp Contest is filled with unexpected situations and heroes.

You already know about Minnesota's Hautman dynasty. Brothers Jim, Bob, and Joe—who grew up a block away from the Coen brothers in St. Louis Park, Minnesota—have won the contest eight times among them since 1989. Joe, a physicist by training, scored the first of his three wins in 1991 and was invited to the White House to be congratulated by President George H. W. Bush. At the time, he had yet to sell a single painting.

Part of the Hautman legend is built on the brothers' attention to duck detail. For example, Joe says, one of his victories came down to a tiebreaker vote between another artist's painting and his painting of a scoter duck. Hautman says he won because one of the judges liked his inclusion of a slight ridge around the bill of his duck. It was the last anatomical detail Hautman added before submitting his entry that year, and he notes without any sense of absurdity that he'd added it after consulting the remains of a dead scoter in his freezer.

Hautman says that, like Berger, he's drawn to the competitive nature of the contest. "The idea of having an anonymously judged contest is pretty appealing to a lot of artists. I went from being a complete unknown to having a name where I can sell thousands of prints and be invited to meet the president. There's nothing else like that in art that I know of."

Berger recounts the legend of Ohio art student Adam Grimm, who in 1999 at the age of twenty-one, became the contest's youngest winner. He entered after his parents agreed that, if he won, they'd let him quit art school to pursue wildlife painting full time. Informed of his victory by phone, Grimm held his parents to their word and quit school immediately.

Berger also mentions avant-garde Minneapolis artist Rob McBroom, whose 2009 entry, his ninth, was just as doomed as the ones he'd submitted before. In a contest where a biologist vets every contender to ensure the biological integrity and correct seasonal plumage of each painted duck, McBroom has become a legend by paying the $125 entry fee each year, then willfully ignoring the clear preference of the judges for realistic scenes. Last year McBroom's painting included rhinestones, and Berger swears the tail feathers of one of McBroom's ducks actually was the Motorola logo.

"It'll never happen, but if I did win I'm sure there would be a lot of pissed-off hunters and philatelic enthusiasts," McBroom told an interviewer in 2008. Contacted for this story, he added, "There's not a whole lot of overlap between wildlife art enthusiasts and the avant-garde art world, so I like to think I'm helping to change that in some small way."

Still, the long-shot promise of fame in the cloistered wildlife art world isn't always enough to sustain the dream. Something far less abstract also is at stake. Says Robert Richert, a Los Alamitos, California, landscape artist who has entered the duck stamp contest almost every year since 1979 and who won the California competition in 1982: "The national recognition overnight can be worth its weight in gold."

Berger and I were pedaling along the San Gabriel River bike path one October morning, engaged in a pointless conversation that's popular among men our age: We were discussing the dicey question of when, or if, we might be able to retire.

While Berger is far too smart to factor income from his art into his retirement calculations, the conversation *did* somehow segue into a discussion of the Federal Duck Stamp Contest judging, which was coming up later that week. A few months earlier, he had e-mailed me a photograph of his entry—a well-composed, nicely detailed acrylic painting of two American wigeons in flight over an autumn marsh, the green-faced drake in the foreground, the less colorful female in the background. The scene is a composite grafted together from a couple of dozen digital photographs Berger took—a wing from one, a retracted foot from another—after luring wintering ducks at that small park in Cypress. "I figured I could spend ten thousand dollars on a big lens," he says, "or ten dollars on a bag of seed."

Now, just days before he prepared to leave for the judging venue just outside Washington, it was clear he'd been imagining possibilities. "Used to be an artist could count on making a million dollars if their duck got picked," he said. "That's not true anymore, but still . . ."

The US Fish and Wildlife Service expends considerable energy stoking such dreams. While the contest offers no cash prize or direct income to the winning artist—the 2009 winner received twenty duck stamps, framed and signed by Interior Secretary Ken Salazar—the brochure notes, "the wildlife artist who wins this competition knows that his or her career and fortunes will take wing!" At least the top twenty-four scoring entries, including the winner, would be "enthusiastically exhibited" throughout the country at museums, festivals, and expositions, and those events are a big draw for collectors and art enthusiasts.

From an artist's point of view, the tour and the stamp are preposterously visible government-subsidized advertisements for the original painting—to which the artist retains all rights—as well as to the artist's other work. Turns out, a lot of hunters, conservationists, and collectors want a limited-edition print of the image that's on the Federal Duck Stamp, and the artist is free to sell as many prints as the market will bear, and to license the image for use on a seemingly endless array of products, from postcards to shower curtains to Christmas ornaments.

Berger entered the 2008 contest after encouragement from two painter friends, duck stamp veterans Richert as well as Robert Copple of Seal Beach, California. Alas, his rendering of a Canada goose that year did not survive a brutal first round of judging. Among the five judges, only two thought Berger's goose worthy of advancing to the second round. He needed three "in" votes to advance. For a competitor like Berger, the challenge intensified. He had promised himself he would enter the contest for three years. Year Two was time to get serious. After a bicycling accident last March laid him up for a few weeks, making it impossible to paint, he spent his down time analyzing the duck stamp equivalent of game films.

"I had a bunch of photos, so I went through and studied the winners," he says. His conclusions? "Two birds is definitely better than one." Birds in flight, rather than simply floating in a pond, seemed more dynamic and might impress the judges. One of the eligible ducks for that year's contest was a wigeon, with patches of bright-green plumage on its head and wings. He settled on that duck because it's common in Southern California and he knew he could take a lot of reference photographs.

Ever the engineer, Berger noticed that, in most of the winning paintings, the background horizon was about one-sixth of the way up from the bottom of the scene. Also, he concluded that simple designs were better, because something too busy would not translate well when the seven-by-ten-inch painting was reduced to stamp size. "I just tried to look for basic things to put mine in the ballpark," he says.

After 130 hours at the living-room easel, his painting was ready. He'd clearly followed the advice of one past winner, which Fisher recalls as "just paint the heck out of the duck" and let the rest of the painting support the lead bird. Still, Berger's strategic bid for one of the art world's most unusual prizes wasn't finished. There was the matter of timing.

Entries are judged anonymously, and in the order in which they're submitted. Berger had noticed that the previous year's winner came from among the early submissions. How would you rather have your duck judged? By jaded judges tired after viewing more than two hundred duck paintings, or among entries presented to still-fresh judges early in the process? He decided he'd be better off submitting his painting well before the August deadline. Among the 224 entries, Berger's was entry thirty-one.

His critical analysis continued through summer and into October, right up to the week of judging. Four days before he traveled to the Maryland wildlife preserve where the entries were to be displayed and judged, Berger pored over a color printout of his competition—his handicapping sheet. Using the conclusions he'd made during his weeks studying the duck contest data, he'd taken a pen and systematically struck through the entries he thought were unlikely to survive the first round. He selected forty-one he thought might represent the toughest competition, and culled that list to the strongest nine, including his among them.

At that point, he figured, he had about a 10 percent chance of becoming the Federal Duck Stamp Artist.

The judging took place on a rainy October weekend at the Patuxent Research Refuge in Laurel, Maryland. For a gathering of people focused on duck paintings, the general mood was serious and intense despite absurdities such as the ritual playing of "Disco Duck" as part of the opening and closing ceremonies, the fake waterfowl dioramas on either side of the judging table, and the angry-looking stuffed goose appended to a reed-festooned podium.

For the most part, the faithful ignored the displays that offered a chance to stroke skunk and raccoon pelts or hold genuine animal skulls. More interesting, it seemed, were the paintings themselves. The room was abuzz with supposed Hautman sightings.

Like Berger, some artists traveled a long way to see how their duck would fare in head-to-head competition. Once there, though, all of Berger's precontest handicapping seemed useless. As he perused his rivals the day before judging, he realized that, despite his careful calculations, his control over the outcome was starting to seem like one of wonderland's illusions. Doubt crept into his voice.

"Winning depends on the subjective whims of five judges who change every year," he said. "So to get into this with the purpose of winning is a little bit crazy. It's a tremendous amount of work, and even if you produce a really nice piece, there's still gotta be some luck."

Amid whispering in the small, dark auditorium, Berger tensed as the judges considered entry thirty-one, his wigeons. Everyone eyed the big, brutal screen where the fate of each painting flashed. By a three-two vote, his painting was "in." His ducks would advance to the next round. Still, eventual winners sometimes get five "in" votes on the first round, and Berger knew instantly that his chance of winning was diminished. Both disappointed and pleased with his progress from the previous year's first-round knockout, he immediately set to work analyzing the vote tallies.

The final judging was scheduled for the next day, and it would be more nuanced. Each of the five judges would assign a score of one to five to each painting, with twenty-five being a perfect score. Only the top five to ten would go to the final round. That night, Berger savored the delicious anticipation of knowing that, in the wild and unpredictable world of competitive duck painting, anything could happen.

The problem with something so wild and unpredictable, of course, is that it's hard to parse the results. On that dreary Saturday in October, only eight entries made it through to the final round—the top five scores, including ties. Berger's wigeons finished with sixteen points, only two points behind one of the two competing Hautmans but well out of the running. Still, like the *Idol* contestant who makes it into the top ten, he finished high enough to be part of the national tour, high enough to spark a steaks-and-wine celebration with friends that night. "A hundred thousand people might see my painting," he said.

The coveted title of Federal Duck Stamp Artist went to fifty-seven-year-old Maryland farmer Robert Bealle. The stamp made from his painting will go on sale in late June, and will show a single, stationary, oddly monochromatic wigeon floating among some reeds. Berger was right about the wigeon being a good choice, and his theory about the advantages of early submission survived intact; Bealle's entry was number fifty. But otherwise Berger's precontest calculations about the appeal of multiple ducks and birds in flight lay in smoking ruins. As for Bealle, who finished second twenty-six years ago and has finished in the top twenty many times, the victory was long-awaited validation.

"I've had a gorilla on my back for twenty-six years," he told the *Baltimore Sun*. "I felt this year if I didn't win it, I was never going to win it."

Berger was philosophical. "I came here thinking I had a small chance to win, so I was a little disappointed when I realized I wasn't going to. But I'm happy I got this far." And he found reason to be encouraged during his post-finals analysis. He was convinced "the judges saw more attributes in mine the second time they saw it. It means I'm on the right track."

This year, Berger says, he's planning to take another crack at the Canada goose. He already has figured out the time of day he wants to depict, as well as the pose. "The painting I did last year had really nice lighting, but not sufficient skill. Now I'm a little further along on the skill."

But there remains a vast divide between those enterprises governed by precise rules, and those that aren't. During his struggle to bridge that gap, Berger feels he learned some valuable lessons.

"I went there thinking it was going to be a crapshoot, and I came back even more convinced it's a crapshoot," he says. "It's very unpredictable, in a relative sense, compared to engineering, so it doesn't make a lot of sense if you're doing it for the purpose of winning. But by competing, I'm becoming a better painter."

Not all of his analysis was for naught, he says. "The top three entries were in my list of the top forty-one. I was able to pick those out. So I can't control everything, but it's possible to predict what might be good enough to win. To be a finalist, that's about as much as I can control."

Ultimately, he says, "If you say it's futile to try to win because it's so unpredictable, I say it also means I *can* win because it's so unpredictable."

In other words, after two years in the competitive duck-painting arena, after getting stomped in 2008 and finishing better during the most recent contest, the rocket scientist doesn't see the pond as half empty, but half full. And in the end, that's enough to keep him going.

POSTSCRIPT

This story is adapted from one that originally appeared in the March 2010 issue of Orange Coast *magazine. Berger continues to compete in the annual duck stamp contest. The magazine story was the basis of Smith's nonfiction book* The Wild Duck Chase, *which later was adapted into a documentary film by Brian Golden Davis called* The Million Dollar Duck. *That film won the Jury and Audience awards at the Slamdance Film Festival in Park City, Utah, in January 2016, and was aired in theaters and on Discovery Communications' Animal Planet in the fall of that year. That exposure helped raise public awareness of the Federal Duck Stamp Program, which continues to support wetlands conservation throughout the United States. More impressive than that, though, is that the 2015 contest saw an unprecedented and historic Hautman brothers sweep, with Joe taking first, Bob second, and Jim third, followed by Jim's first-place finish in the 2016 contest.*

Chapter Thirteen

Woofers on Wheels

Cruising for chicks with the self-proclaimed "King of Sound Pressure" aboard a mostly undriveable minitruck that can make your ears bleed (1989)

Forget practicality. That's not the point. The point, explains the self-proclaimed "King of Sound Pressure," is to boom. *BOOOOOOOOOOOM!* Rattle windows. Turn heads. Wake the dead. Let every babe within the considerable earshot of your truck know, frankly, that yours is the biggest.

"Remember horsepower back in the Sixties?" shouts the king, Bill Harrill, as he cranks his white-on-blue 1985 Nissan pickup to life. "Why did people put that much horsepower in their cars? It's the same with boom trucks. He who is loudest is king."

With that, Harrill eases his low-slung truck over a speed bump— *SCREEEEEEECH!*—and into traffic along Stanton Avenue in Buena Park, a community in Orange County just south of Los Angeles. The vehicle is stylish but grotesque, a custom-painted 2,200-pound minitruck moving sluggishly beneath the weight of a 1,200-pound audio system. With wide tires that look nearly flat and a specially lowered frame that's less than two inches off the ground, it looks less like the envy of Southern California's peculiar minitruck subculture than an overburdened pack animal.

"It rides great on level ground, but bumps and dips and curbs are a little bit of a hassle," says the Anaheim resident, slowing almost to a stop

Bill "King of Sound Pressure" Harrill in the back of his boom truck before crossing a railroad track. "But once you get going, it's as smooth as can be."

To facilitate conversation, the twenty-four-year-old Harrill momentarily mutes the audio beast that so far has won him twenty-six trophies, including a four-and-a-half-foot-tall number commemorating his victory in a "Bass Most Likely to Kill" contest staged by a truck club called Seductive Minis. At full volume, his sound system's concussive 132-decibel beat can rearrange the hairstyle of anyone in the cab, make it difficult for them to breathe, and, if cranked without protection, cause permanent ear damage.

To pedestrians and other motorists, the approach of Harrill's truck might feel like a rumbling realignment of the Whittier Narrows fault.

"At a hundred and twenty decibels, it really starts to physically hit you," says Harrill, a car audio technician. "You can feel it in your heart. It vibrates your skin."

Even in silence, Harrill's creation is intimidating. For example, while the truck itself runs on only one standard automotive battery, its audio system requires four rechargeable deep-cycle marine batteries. Its sixteen amplifiers generate the equivalent of 3,300 watts of power to drive twelve bass-belching, fifteen-inch woofer speakers in the truck bed, a dozen ten-inch woofers mounted behind the seats (to communicate the sonic boom directly to the passengers' spines), and thirty-two mid-range and high-frequency speakers wedged into every available nook of the cab, including seven in each of the two doors.

"I've cracked windows. I've cracked the camper shell," Harrill says. "You know the handles on the back of the shell? They rattled completely off."

Once a month, he has to retighten the truck's bolts.

Control panels cram the dashboard, which includes an AM-FM cassette deck, a compact disc player with a ten-disc changer, a videocassette recorder with a four-and-a-half-inch color screen, and a drum machine Harrill uses to make his own boom music during slow periods at car shows and audio competitions.

All in all, Harrill has rebuilt the system seventeen times. Counting the fifteen hundred hours he spent working on it, he figures he has spent about forty thousand dollars on a truck that cost him ten-thousand dollars new. Nonetheless, he relies on a relatively puny five-band graphic equalizer to control his audio reproduction. Accuracy is for audiophiles. This is knuckle-sandwich sound.

And that, Harrill is certain, is what women want.

"It's pure sex," says William Burton, editor of Sherman Oaks–based *Car Audio and Electronics* magazine. "It's a male competition to attract nubile eighteen-year-olds. In the Sixties, power was under your hood. Now you're talking about the power in your trunk. But what we're really talking about is the power in your shorts."

So the secret is out. The adolescent love affair with cars and music has warped into what Anaheim-based *Truckin'* and *Minitruckin'* magazines call "this megawatt and mega-thump-thump stereo fad." But as a cultural phenomenon, it's a little more complicated.

Boom truckers borrow from several cultures. From the Hispanic low-riders, they take their street-hugging suspensions and special tires. From black rap musicians, they borrow the heavy bass beat that makes them go boom. And as a result, thousands of mostly white kids have in the past five years created a whole new arena in which to measure their machismo.

In the days before manufacturers began sponsoring organized car audio competitions with precise sound-measuring instruments, boom truckers gathered at intersections where the streetlights were rigged with earthquake sensors. The boom truckers discovered that the sensors—designed to cut power to the high-voltage street lights in case they should fall during an earthquake—were a reasonably reliable way to test the power of their audio systems.

"They'd crank it up until they could turn the streetlight off," says Burton. If they were successful, Burton says the boom truckers would drive a few yards away from the light and try it again. "They'd keep doing it until they found a point where they couldn't turn the light off anymore. That's how they would judge."

Today, the Car Audio National competition—considered by many the best-organized audio contest—has a 132-page judge's guide and a standard compact disc designed to push sound systems to their limits. On the disc: Duke Ellington, Glenn Miller, Billy Cobham, Jennifer Warnes, and others. Judges test for frequency response and sound pressure (decibel level), but also judge the wiring, intent of vehicle use, integrity of component installation, cosmetic integration, ease of use, attention to detail, and general creativity. The criteria for judging sound quality include staging, stereo imaging, definition and clarity of frequency range, and the absence of unintended noise.

"The whole car stereo competition idea is the Eighties version of drag racing in souped-up cars in the Fifties," says Jim Wunderlich, public relations director for the car audio division of Alpine Electronics in Torrance, sponsor of the Car Audio National competition. "Our judging is very specific. We want to hear the most impressive sound system without having to see it. And we don't want boom-boom-boom. People with overbearing bass on their system get points off, and that upsets a lot of kids."

An estimated two hundred fifty minitruck clubs now represent thousands of members registered with the Southern California Mini Truck Council, according to Jason Sanabia of Buena Park, and council membership has gone up 50 percent in the past two years. But it's hardly a unified front. Even among other minitruck enthusiasts, boom truckers are acknowledged as a different breed.

"The rage in minitrucks is to lower them, to make them look clean, and of course, it's not complete until you have that booming sound," says twenty-six-year-old Eric Holdaway, whose Speaker Works in Orange stresses audio quality over loudness. "They're mostly kids who want to roll down the street and call attention to themselves. Whether or not that's antisocial behavior, I'll leave up to you."

While audio purists describe Harrill and his ilk as electronics abusers, plenty of wannabes are hauling massive audio systems around Sun Belt states such as California, Texas, and Florida.

"In our own customer files, we probably have over six hundred trucks with at least two thousand dollars' worth of audio equipment in them," says Harrill, a technician for Audio Chamber in Buena Park, where many boom truck owners do their dreaming. "We have twenty trucks with over seven thousand dollars in them, and five trucks with over ten thousand."

Car audio retailers such as Holdaway, Harrill, and Audio Chamber's Richard Shen marvel at the willingness of customers—almost always young men between the ages of sixteen and twenty-five—to spend lavishly on equipment that can produce decibel levels similar to those generated by jet engines and chain saws. "It's really hard to believe," Harrill says. "Some of them save up. Some of them get it from their parents. We've had sixteen-year-old kids walk in with thousands of dollars in cash."

Sanabia, the twenty-four-year-old director for the California Cruizers club, pleads guilty. "I never intended it to go this far, but you get caught up," he says of his 1986 Nissan, which sports a vanity plate reading "SO DEF." "First, I just wanted four speakers and a radio, but then I sat in [Harrill's] truck. You get hungry. You get involved in competitions. Now I have a better stereo in my truck than I have at home."

"Most guys in trucks, all they want is a big square box in the bed with a bunch of woofers," says Dan Kuhns of Anaheim, whose 1987 Mazda minitruck placed fourth in the 750 watts or less division at the Car Audio Nationals championship last October. That contest emphasizes sound and installation quality over loudness. "It's just like the old hot rods. They want lots of noise. They stuff speakers anywhere they can fit them."

While boom truckers might be audio outlaws, few can ever hope to achieve Harrill's level of, well, volume. He wins recognition in the sound pressure competition at car audio shows, and that, apparently, is what matters to him. Besides, Harrill reached a pop culture pinnacle of sorts when his truck was featured in the music video for a song by L'Trimm titled "Cars With the Boom."

SCRUUUUUUUUNCH! A culvert. Harrill drives on, conceding that his truck represents audio overkill. "I did it to show people what can be done," he says, just before, again, suggesting a more primal motive. "But it's definitely for impressing the women."

Burton, the audio magazine editor, agrees. "You know, the vibrations from these things can be very stimulating. You have to agree that music is probably more addictive than cocaine. People use it to get excited, relax, to party. It has an incredible emotional effect." From rap to rock, he says, music is a universal language. "And the relationship between sex and rock 'n' roll goes way back. Dancing is just the vertical expression of a horizontal desire."

But does it work?

"Oh yeah," says Harrill. "That's the problem. I always wonder whether it's me or the truck."

There are more obvious drawbacks. The sound equipment in Harrill's truck is worth eighteen thousand dollars, he says, and he pays fourteen hundred dollars a year to insure it. He won't eat in restaurants where he can't see his truck from the window. The special tires, which help give his truck its low, clean profile, add to the awkwardness of the ride. "Yeah, it's a little more stiff with them, but we sacrifice because it looks better."

Hauling around his audio system required some changes under the hood. Nissan's standard 110-horsepower engine proved inadequate, so Harrill added an extra carburetor and rebuilt the exhaust system and cylinder head to help boost the horsepower to about 150. Around town, the once-economical minitruck now gets between twelve and eighteen miles per gallon. And at the moment, Harrill says the truck isn't even street legal because the headlights are too low.

As he scrapes across the slight rise at the base of his mother's driveway, Harrill explains that this is where he parks his other two trucks, a relatively stock 1987 Toyota and a 1974 Datsun. He finally admits that his boom truck is best suited for audio competitions and is far too impractical for everyday use. Still:

"It's the urge for being the biggest and doing it best."

POSTSCRIPT

This essay is adapted from a piece published in the January 23, 1989, issue of the Orange County Register. *The young man's biological imperative to invest heavily in what, essentially, is an absurd and desperate mating call continues, though according to Jeremy Cook, the editor of* Truckin' *magazine: "It evolves, like anything else." Since this story appeared, the size of audio equipment needed to produce that booming sound has shrunk. "Digital amps now fit under the seats," he says. iPods, smartphones, and other personal electronics also changed the dynamic. At the same time, the trucks have gotten bigger. "The last true minitruck was the 2011 Ford Ranger. Technically, they're all mid-size now."* Minitruckin' *magazine folded in 2014. The earsplitters have segmented off into their own subculture, separate and distinct from more mainstream truck enthusiasts who these days are focused on tire size and air-ride systems that allow vehicles to ride so low they look like vacuum cleaners. That's not to say the boom truckers left no mark on truck culture. Cook says boom trucks "kinda went away, but even so, you don't call a show truck complete these days unless is has a great sound system."*

CHAPTER FOURTEEN

Buzz Aldrin's Traveling Tube of Glue

The Apollo 11 *hero landed hard when he came back to Earth, which makes the fragile toothpick model in his travel bag all the more poignant (1989)*

THE PACIFIC COAST SLIPS PAST BUZZ ALDRIN'S LIMOUSINE WINDOW IN the murky blur of a recent dawn. The former astronaut's mood is good despite the early hour, the day's hectic book-tour schedule, and the prospect of facing another stream of interviewers who want to know, basically, how it feels to be one of the first men on the moon.

It's not that the Laguna Beach, California, resident is uncomfortable with his past or the acclaim that endures twenty years after the historic flight of *Apollo 11*. During this marathon day in San Diego, he would cheerfully interrupt a hurried meal five times to sign autographs for starstruck Coco's customers and waitresses. It's just that, with the approach of Thursday's twentieth anniversary of the first moon landing, the silver-haired, square-jawed Aldrin is looking ahead.

While debate drags on about a proposed space station, he sees a time when a modular spaceport cycles in an elliptical orbit between Earth and Mars; when Earth's energy needs are met by helium-3 shipped from the moon aboard interplanetary cargo vessels; and when vacationing families can visit a museum on the moon's Tranquility Base and see the footprints left by Aldrin, now fifty-nine, and fellow *Apollo 11* astronaut Neil Armstrong.

"We can sit back and look at how great it was, or we can look forward with vision and see how maybe it can be in the future," Aldrin says, and his blue eyes begin to roam the horizon. "I think nations that live in the past are pretty sad, and that's certainly not where I want to be as an individual."

The Buzz Aldrin familiar to most Southern California residents is what *People* magazine recently called "a prized peacock" on the local social circuit. With his third wife, Lois Driggs Aldrin, he often appears at high-profile functions wearing his Air Force dress uniform bedecked with ribbons and the unmistakable aura of a living legend. To an entire generation, the familiar image of Aldrin saluting the American flag on the lunar surface represents a rare moment when there seemed no limits. Even as the United States struggled with Vietnam and civil rights, Aldrin, Armstrong, and crewmate Michael Collins floated above it all like oracles.

But the same man turning heads at local parties and charity events also is the technically brilliant, intensely self-analytical, and sometimes troubled man who colleagues describe as "an original thinker . . . not bound by whatever is politically fashionable" and, perhaps consequently, "a frustrated visionary." Former NASA administrator Thomas Paine considers him "a prophet crying in the wilderness."

"Neither the country nor his compatriots who remained at NASA are quite ready for Buzz's ideas," says Paine, a Santa Monica–based space consultant who was chairman of President Reagan's National Commission on Space. "But in the end, I think he'll prevail. He's convinced he's right, and he probably is."

To those unfamiliar with Aldrin's almost evangelical crusade for a renewed commitment to space exploration, his talk of interplanetary travel and the failure of American will since Apollo makes him seem more like Buck Rogers with an attitude. What Aldrin has been saying in radio and TV appearances, speeches, and in his new book *Men From Earth*, is that the United States should not have abandoned the space exploration it began with the Apollo missions. He says the space agency that pulled off a lunar landing eight years after President Kennedy issued

Buzz Aldrin at the San Diego Aero-Space Museum during a commemoration of the 20th anniversary of the first moon landing
RICK RICKMAN, THE *ORANGE COUNTY REGISTER*, JULY 16, 1989. USED WITH PERMISSION.

his famous challenge has been sapped of its vitality, leadership, funding, and goals.

On that, at least, even some NASA insiders agree.

"In everybody's minds, the Apollo years were the golden years," says Frank Martin, NASA's assistant administrator for exploration. "NASA could do no wrong. There was a lot of money—four to five percent of the federal budget at one time, whereas now it's one percent—but the whole country's attitude toward technology has changed. We tend to back away from it now."

Not Aldrin. He openly criticizes the untapped potential of the space shuttle program. Using the incredibly sophisticated shuttle to place satellites into Earth's orbit is the equivalent of delivering mail in a Ferrari Testarosa, Aldrin and other critics say.

"There was a lot left to prove," says Aldrin, whose pioneering doctoral work in orbital mechanics at MIT forms the groundwork for the space rendezvous procedures used today. "Why didn't we use this great team we put together? Why didn't we use this technical marvel called the Saturn V? Why didn't we use the pioneering work on cryogenic liquid hydrogen [rocket fuel] that really enabled us to get to the moon? . . . There are so many things we could have done to capitalize on what we achieved."

As a self-styled space futurist occasionally working as a consultant to NASA subcontractors, Aldrin pushes for a national commitment to explore Mars using a spaceport, a sort of orbiting bus station that uses the gravitational pull of Earth and Mars to shuttle landing craft between the two planets. He also wants to see solar power captured on the moon and microwaved back to Earth, and a "negotiated non-race" between the United States and the Soviet Union that would combine scarce resources and share credit for future space successes.

"If I can get people to understand what I'm trying to say and understand the long-range impact of it," Aldrin says, "to me that's worth the personal sacrifice of being criticized as a maverick, a troublemaker, or a loose cannon, whatever that is."

If that indeed is Aldrin's reputation—and there are those within the space community who agree with his self-assessment—its roots extend to Aldrin's earliest days in the space program. He was a Korean War fighter pilot who, in 1959, decided to take a nontraditional route to the astronaut corps. Aldrin enrolled at MIT to specialize in spacecraft rendezvous, gambling that NASA eventually would drop the requirement that astronauts be test pilots. In 1963, he dedicated his thesis, "Line of Sight Guidance Techniques for Manned Orbital Rendezvous," to "the men in the astronaut program. Oh that I were one of them."

NASA finally dropped the requirement and Aldrin's application for the program was accepted. The young pilot was "out of my head with excitement," according to *Return to Earth*, Aldrin's 1973 autobiography, but from the start he shouldered the role of the outsider. As one of original scientist-astronauts among the program's "right stuff" fighter jocks, Aldrin sometimes was derided as "Dr. Rendezvous." His potential value to the Gemini and Apollo programs did not go unrecognized by NASA decision makers, though, and in 1966 he flew aboard *Gemini 12*—the last and one of the most successful flights of the two-man mission era.

Even as it became clear that Aldrin would be chosen for the *Apollo 11* mission, the first lunar landing, he found himself wishing what other astronauts would have considered sacrilegious—to be assigned a different flight. "Not only would there be considerably less public attention," he wrote in *Return to Earth*, "but a later flight would be more complicated, more adventurous, and a far greater test of my abilities than the first landing."

Aldrin's concern about the lack of adventure proved somewhat valid, although the first landing in the spidery lunar module—dubbed *Eagle*—was a Hollywood-style cliffhanger. Aldrin and Armstrong eased the lander into the moon dust with less than twenty seconds of fuel left, prompting their radio contact in Houston to greet word of the touchdown by saying, "You've got a bunch of guys about to turn blue. We're breathing again. Thanks a lot."

But the ensuing twenty-four hours on the lunar surface, while impossibly romantic for the billion or so who watched the grainy TV transmissions, were for Aldrin and Armstrong a series of tedious chores and mundane concerns—picking up rocks, setting up experiments, taking pictures, worrying about whether the flag was planted firmly and whether the coiled TV cable near their spacecraft eventually would ensnare one or the other.

"If you were pontificating about what it all meant, you were just liable to trip," Aldrin says.

His concern about the intensity of public attention proved particularly prophetic. The public acclaim that greeted the *Apollo 11* crew upon its return only complicated Aldrin's search for a niche within the space agency. He was too famous for a low-level spot and too inexperienced for a top job, so after a yearlong world tour doing public relations for NASA, Aldrin returned to the Air Force a hero without goals.

"I wanted to ease my way back in by becoming commandant of the cadets at the Air Force Academy," he says, "but apparently someone else was being groomed for that. Then there was an aeronautical wind-tunnel job at Wright-Patterson, but somehow that didn't seem quite right. So they finally said, 'Why don't you command the test-pilot school?' Well, in the absence of any other ideas on my part, that's what I settled on doing," he says—a decision that aggravated an already dangerous personal situation.

Aldrin had struggled with self-doubt and depression after *Apollo 11*, and his performance at the test-pilot school was not up to his demanding standards. Two years after the moon mission, he acknowledged his depression to Air Force superiors and thought that "coming to grips with those problems and moving on would not adversely affect my chances for promotion to general. I was dead wrong."

When he talks about his troubled personal odyssey, Aldrin speaks with the same candor that led him to reveal in *Return to Earth* a prolonged extramarital affair that was unraveling his first marriage; his family's history of depression and suicide; and the fact that he was "the first man to pee in his pants on the moon." He now describes the 1973 book as a misguided attempt to regain control of his life two years after seeking help for depression and five years before confronting his problem with alcohol.

"Obviously, it was a premature time to say, 'Gee, I think I've got a handle on what's troubling me,'" says Aldrin, who credits Alcoholics Anonymous for his past ten years of sobriety. "What was troubling me was a genetic tendency enhanced by a lot of exterior events. The book ended on an uncertain note, hopefully optimistic. Well, it got worse."

It's difficult to find friends or professional colleagues who remember much contact with Aldrin during the mid and late 1970s, and Aldrin prefers not to elaborate on his allusion to events during that time. "If I had really wanted to get into depth discussions of that, I would have put it in *Men From Earth*," he says. "And I can't really discuss what happened there without violating the traditions of Alcoholics Anonymous."

What's clear, though, is that the Buzz Aldrin who reemerged in the early 1980s was a changed man, a determined man, and a man, finally, with a mission. He began appearing at space conferences that had names such as "A Case for Mars." He moved to Laguna Beach from Brentwood in 1985 so he could be closer to major aerospace contractors and fellow visionaries at the California Space Institute at the University of California, San Diego. And spurred by the energetic Lois, whom he met in 1986 and married last year, Aldrin also began taking his case to the public.

Aldrin's effect as a figurehead in the back-to-the-future movement remains uncertain. He has no illusions about the glacial pace of government decision making, and he also understands that the days of exploration for the sake of exploration probably are gone forever.

"We won't see it again in the same naïve, single-purpose way as when Columbus and Magellan said, 'Hey I want to go do this,'" he says. "It's got to be for a lot more particular reason."

Some, including Aldrin, feel the "loose cannon" reputation might work against him. He recalled a time two years ago when he offered his expertise to two large defense companies angling for the $1.9-billion space-station contract, which in December 1988 was awarded to McDonnell Douglas. "They acknowledged my potential value," he says, "but the gist of a comment from one of them was, 'We can't hire you. It might jeopardize the possibility of us winning the space-station award.'"

Others also sense the space industry's arm's-length attitude toward Aldrin. "To be perfectly frank, Buzz had some problems after *Apollo 11*," says Louis Friedman, former manager of advanced studies at the Jet Propulsion Laboratory in Pasadena and the executive director of the 125,000-member Planetary Society, the largest private space-interest group in the world. "That already is an image problem for the system and NASA to deal with. One of their guys with the 'right stuff' wasn't really perfect. The other thing is that he's not controllable. He does and says what he thinks, even if it's not technically popular. And that makes people uncomfortable. . . . He's so dogged that people on the inside shy away from him."

Still, the grapevine at NASA and within the aerospace industry is filled with rumors that President Bush plans to use Thursday's twentieth anniversary of the *Apollo 11* moon landing to make a major announcement about the space program. Although the White House would not confirm the rumors, many consider them a hopeful sign.

Nonetheless, Aldrin was a relentless salesman as his limousine headed south that recent day. He unzipped a travel bag on the seat beside him and removed a box containing a foot-tall model of a "segmented tetrahedron." What Aldrin considers a logical design for his envisioned spaceport looked more like a fragile toothpick sculpture doomed to be crushed in transit—a fate many say will befall many of Aldrin's ideas.

But the important thing to remember about Aldrin, at least at this stage of his life, is that he carries glue in his briefcase.

POSTSCRIPT

This essay is adapted from a profile that first appeared in the July 16, 1989, edition of the Orange County Register. *Aldrin has continued to write books and criticize NASA for its timidity in space exploration, and in 2013 revealed to an audience at the Florida Institute of Technology a "master plan" he hoped NASA would adopt that involved colonizing Mars within twenty-five years, and establishing a settlement there by 2040. He also has become a ubiquitous figure in popular culture, teaming with Snoop Dogg and Quincy Jones on the rap single and video "Rocket Experience," appearing on* The Big Bang Theory, *and voicing a parody version of himself on* The Simpsons.

Chapter Fifteen

The Mark of Mickey

Exploring a Disneyland archive filled with photos of the iconic three-circle silhouette of Mickey Mouse's head as it occurs randomly in nature (1992)

ITEM: SAGE VAN ANTWERP WAS BORN MARCH 1, 1991, THE NORMAL fourth child of Steve and Lorie Van Antwerp of Sister Lakes, Michigan. But the first time her parents changed Sage's diaper, they knew right away: She bore the mark.

Item: On New Year's Day this year, a litter of piglets was born to a sloppy-fat sow in Berwick, Pennsylvania. There, plain as day on one piglet's upturned belly—the mark!

Item: A rancher in Victoria, Texas, noticed the mark on one of his four-year-old female crossbred longhorns. As the beast grazed beneath a spreading tree, the rancher crept as close as he dared and fired off a half a roll of film.

The rancher's pictures and hundreds of similarly unique photographs now reside in Diane Turner's "Mickey Markings" file, where the Disneyland publicist keeps correspondence from anyone who perceives, and then takes a picture of, the familiar three-circle silhouette of Mickey Mouse's head as it occurs randomly in nature.

The Central Intelligence Agency may keep more sensitive files, but none could be more entertaining.

Mickey among the spots of dozens of Dalmatians. Mickey in the furry underbelly of a pot-bellied pig. A Mickey-shaped stand of untended trees on a distant hillside. Mickey on a pair of snakeskin cowboy boots. A Mickey-shaped coffee spill stain on an interoffice memo. Mickey-shaped garden tomatoes, potato chips, ginger roots, cacti, and barnacle clusters. A Mickey-shaped potato its Nebraska grower pledged to "preserve in my refrigerator in case I do hear from you."

And, of course, the Mickey-shaped birthmark on Sage Van Antwerp's dimpled bottom.

"At first I had them broken down by animal, vegetable, and mineral," says Turner, who has collected and filed hundreds of incoming photographs since taking over the duty sixteen months ago. "But we get so many, now I have it broken down by dogs, cats, livestock, vegetable, and mineral. The baby comes under livestock, I'm sad to say."

The envelopes arrive from all over the country, steadily and without invitation, often by registered mail. They're stuffed with photographic proof of the apparition and testimonials that seem equal parts spiritual rapture and *Weekly World News* lead story.

The Mickey mark can turn up anywhere, including this rock formation.
ISTOCKPHOTO BY GETTY IMAGES BY KITCHAKRON, 2015, USED WITH PERMISSION

Some are savvy, such as the Texas rancher who wrote: "Being part longhorn, she would make a great addition to your Wild West Show at EuroDisney." Some are sad, such as the Lucerne Valley woman who wrote: "My kids have never been to Disneyland because we just don't have the money. But they talk about it all the time. When our dog had puppies, they were so happy that one had a Mickey Mouse picture on her."

Does Disney want to buy a three-week-old Mickey-marked lamb? "It is for sale if anyone is interested," wrote an Iowa farmer. Any interest in a brown-and-white dog named Brit with a Mickey mark between her ears? "We do not want to sell her but are willing to let her be used for publicity," wrote a Las Vegas couple.

The recent outpouring may have been spurred in 1988 when Disneyland began promoting "Mickey Moo," a Mickey-marked Holstein dairy cow that is part of the Big Thunder Ranch attraction in Frontierland. But Turner and Disney archivists say similar photos have been arriving for decades.

Why? It's anyone's guess. Novelist John Updike describes Mickey Mouse as the perfect symbol for "America as it feels to itself—plucky, put-on, inventive, resilient, good-natured, game." Perhaps people see in Mickey markings a chance to capture on film a reflection of this society's soul?

Nah. A little too ponderous.

Maybe, as communications professors Susan G. Davis of the University of California, San Diego, says, finding a Mickey marking is a suitable substitute for those in far-flung locales who can't participate in the "ritual obligation" of visiting a Disney theme park. "There's a sense that you don't really participate in the larger culture until you go to this place, see these things, wear that sweatshirt, or have that on your wristwatch," says Davis, who is writing a book on theme parks. "It's really approaching the level where there's a sense of deprivation if you don't partake and participate in it."

Or perhaps, as visual communications expert Brian Stonehill of Pomona College says, people are simply fascinated by "things that lie on the boundary between what's meaningful and what's random. It's the sense of nature teasing us by giving us these things. People search for any little nugget of meaning and warmth in what otherwise would seem to be random markings of nature."

Whatever.

Turner tries to follow up, congratulating the letter writers by mail and occasionally sending breathless news releases to hometown newspapers. But in truth, no one ever got rich or famous thanks to the Mickey markings on their fruits, vegetables, and household pets. And eventually, practical realities intrude, as it did with the Canoga Park woman who sent a picture of "Sweet Pea," her Mickey-marked steer. Turner eventually got a grim update, and it's reflected in the note she wrote to herself on the envelope bearing Sweet Pea's picture:

"Bought & slaughtered."

POSTSCRIPT

This essay is adapted from one that appeared June 23, 1992, in the Orange County Register. *There's no reason to believe that people have stopped projecting Mickey markings onto animals, vegetables, or minerals, though a current Disneyland publicist found no evidence that anyone at the Anaheim, California, theme park continues to maintain a file of those submissions. Perhaps people these days are content to post such sightings on their Facebook pages or Instagram accounts rather than alerting the Walt Disney Company about them.*

Chapter Sixteen

The Downside of Perfection

At a time when style trumps everything, a seventy-something Long Beach, California, podiatrist sets out to master the most boring shot in basketball (1998)

In January 1992, a retired sixty-nine-year-old podiatrist began showing up at the Rossmoor Athletic Club in Los Alamitos every morning at 5:30. He'd park his Chrysler in the dark lot, pull a bulky gym bag from the trunk, and shuffle past the disinterested front-desk clerk. He'd climb a steep staircase, huff across a catwalk, and down another steep staircase, headed for the basketball court he knew would be empty.

His name was Tom Amberry. The guy was big, six-foot-five, pushing two-sixty, and desperately out of shape. Some mornings, he'd forget to ask the desk clerk to turn on the lights in the gym. Rather than risk a heart attack by climbing all those stairs again, he'd just open the doors into the dim artificial light of the hallway, pull a basketball from his bag, and step up to the line for the first of the five hundred free throws he shot each day.

Amberry carried twenty pennies in his left pants pocket. After twenty-five shots, he'd move a penny to his right pocket. After a hundred shots, he'd walk to his gym bag, pull out a small notebook, and log how many of those one hundred shots he'd made. Then back to the line for another hundred. Back and forth he'd go, as consistent as a machine, until all twenty pennies were in his right pocket. He'd log his final shots in the notebook, pack his bag, and go home for a nap.

Tom Amberry mastered one of sports' most deceptively complex challenges.
PHOTO BY CON KEYES © 1995 *LOS ANGELES TIMES.* USED WITH PERMISSION.

No one paid Amberry much mind until nearly two years later when, on November 15, 1993, at the age of seventy-one, he stepped up to that same foul line in front of witnesses from the Guinness Book of Records and shot free throws for twelve straight hours, 2,750 times, without missing once. At lot of people noticed him then, but oddly, not the people who should have.

As impressive as Amberry's world record is, it begs for some perspective. He did not cure a deadly disease, negotiate a lasting world peace, or solve any of the major problems that confound the human race. What he did, though, was perfect the mechanics and mentality of shooting an unopposed free throw—tossing a basketball through a stationary, ten-foot-high iron hoop from fifteen feet away. In doing so, Amberry mastered one of the most unique and deceptively complex challenges in sports.

"When you shoot a free throw, the only thing between you and the basket is yourself," Amberry wrote in *Free Throw: Seven Steps to Success at the Free Throw Line*, a book he coauthored with Philip Reed in 1996. "You stand alone on that line with just your muscles, your heart, and your beliefs. If you miss, you get all the blame. If you make it, you deserve all the glory."

The apparent simplicity of the task is at the center of what Biola University basketball coach Jim Poteet calls "the paradox of the free throw."

"Think about it," says fifty-seven-year-old Poteet, who has chosen Amberry's free throw shooting method as the topic of his doctoral dissertation at Oklahoma State University. "There's this hectic basketball game going on. Then there's a foul. All of a sudden, the player in that hectic pace is, in fifteen seconds, asked to change his whole mental and physical approach to the game and shoot a free throw. It's tough physiologically because his heart is racing. But it's even tougher psychologically."

Other sports have deceptively simple challenges—football's field goal, golf's four-foot putt, soccer's penalty kick—but Poteet and sports psychologists agree that no other sport offers the full-speed-to-dead-stop mental challenge of a free throw. "Football comes close with the field goal, but the field goal kicker is a specialist," Poteet says. "He's not in the flow of the game before he does his thing. But every player on a basketball court is going to have to shoot free throws."

More and more often, in both college gyms and National Basketball Association arenas, they're missing. As the full-court game became more fluid and intuitive, the science of free throw shooting—a skill that requires mechanical consistency and intense concentration rather than free-form artistic expression—began a slow but steady decline. *The Official Men's College Basketball Records Book*, which has tracked college free throw shooting since 1948, shows a steady rise in player accuracy as balls and backboards improved. That percentage peaked in 1979 at 69.7 percent.

Then it started raining bricks. The free throw percentage fell just as steadily as it had risen, sinking to 67.4 percent in 1997. Female college players watched their free throw percentage drop from 67.3 percent in 1992 to 66.4 percent last year.

Among pro players, the drop has been more dramatic. Those high-flying millionaire gland cases whose midair acrobatics dominate the highlight films can't seem to shoot standing still. As the NBA season winds down, statisticians expect the average free throw percentage among pros in 1997–1998 to be less than 73 percent—an astonishing 3.6 percent decline in the past nine seasons. If the numbers seem small, remember that free throws usually account for more than 20 percent of the points scored in games, and they almost always represent the difference between winning and losing.

Players, coaches, and fans know how important free throws are, and nothing frustrates them more than wasted opportunities. But the slide continues, and the search goes on for a way to turn it around.

The greatest free throw shooter in history eases his size fourteen Filas beneath a snack bar table after his regular morning workout, which these days he begins at a more leisurely 8 a.m. Amberry's a trim 210 pounds now, about what he weighed during the 1946–47 season when as a center he led the nation's college players in scoring. He's a bit hard of hearing but still the same generous guy. Occasionally, he used to buy office equipment for his residents who were setting up their own practices, and he donates money to the California College of Podiatric Medicine in San Francisco, from which he graduated in 1951.

Despite his age and accomplishments, Amberry seldom plays the philosopher's role. Ask him his secret, and he says, "All you do is focus on what you're doing at the time you're doing it. Put all distractions out of your mind and have one goal: Put the ball in the basket. That's all you do."

The ritual Amberry follows at the free throw line is only slightly more elaborate. The more you watch him, the more you understand the essential secret of his success both during his forty years as a surgeon and as a postretirement free throw shooter: In an operating room or at the free throw line, everything you do should have a purpose.

"Tom can concentrate and focus on what needs to be done better than anybody I've ever met," says fellow Long Beach podiatrist Eric Hubbard, who trained under Amberry during his residency. "He has a system for doing almost everything."

For example, he says, as a foot surgeon Amberry was able to radically reduce surgery times by refining and systematizing his techniques. "Everything from the way you pick up the instruments to where you make the incision," says Hubbard, whom Amberry credits with first coaxing him back onto the basketball court a couple of weeks after he retired. "Don't waste time. Don't talk. If you have to use a certain type of blade, use it for everything you need it to do before you put it down."

Amberry's surgical innovations were the result of what he calls "time-and-motion studies," and Hubbard says those innovations helped Amberry "refine his surgeries to the point where he could do them much faster than anyone had ever seen."

As a free throw shooter, Amberry is just as methodical. After clearing his mind, he places his feet square to the line—an unstylish pose seemingly lifted from a long-forgotten basketball textbook. He grasps the ball exactly the same way for each shot, focusing his concentration on the ball's inflation hole. With both hands, he bounces the ball three times, thunk-thunk-thunk, no more, no less. Elbows close to his sides, knees bent, he offers a quick glance at the hoop and shoots a one-handed set shot in a high arc toward the basket. Swish.

Watching Amberry is about as exciting as watching an assembly line, but the results are just as consistent. By shooting exactly the same way each time, he minimizes the physical and psychological variables that can send a shot left or right, too long or too short. That can be especially important when the pressure is on during close games.

To those who argue that shooting in a quiet gym is not the same as shooting for the win in front of thousands of screaming fans, Amberry offers his own accomplishments as proof. In February 1997, he shot 374 free throws in a row without missing during an hourlong television show on Fox. He shot 306 in a row in forty-two minutes during a show on Nashville's TNN. During a segment of the television show *Ordinary Extraordinary* with host John Ritter last summer, Amberry sank ten straight while Ritter, the studio audience, and even chesty sports distraction Morgana the Kissing Bandit tried to rattle him.

"The person with the most to lose is under the greatest pressure," he wrote in his book. "Right now, I'm the world's greatest free throw shooter. If someone challenges me and I lose, I've lost the world championship."

Despite everything, some remain unconvinced. "Sometimes I work with college players, and they don't want to follow the steps," Amberry says. "They say, 'Hey, my style got me here.' I think that ten years ago, with more games on TV, it became more of a style thing. So I just ask them, 'Do you want to look good, or do you want to score points?'"

The answer is painfully obvious. While free throws may win games, they almost never make the highlight films. So Amberry is finding it hard to convince high-flying college and NBA superstars to shoot like a seventy-five-year-old podiatrist.

"If Dr. Tom had developed the equivalent method for golf, a way to sink every six-foot putt, he would be a multimillionaire by now. He'd spend all his time teaching the pros," says Reed, with whom Amberry collaborated on his book. "But pro basketball players and colleges act as if he doesn't exist. They're in denial about how bad free throw shooting is."

Hubbard agrees. "The pros now are a different culture than they were twenty or thirty years ago. There are players getting twenty million dollars a year. They've all got contracts with sponsors. Everybody is trying to get something from them. The attitude of some of these guys is that nobody can teach them anything. But any pro that had an opportunity to work with Tom would benefit. He spent three hours teaching me, and now I can shoot fifty in a row. How many pro players can shoot fifty in a row?"

In a letter last year nominating Amberry to the Naismith Memorial Basketball Hall of Fame, hall-of-famer Pete Newell, now a scout with the Cleveland Cavaliers, wrote: "In a game that seems to have [fewer] teachers than any time in the last half century, we need Dr. Tom to bring more teaching back into the game. As described in a magazine article a decade ago, 'the game is overcoached and undertaught.' Let us recognize the importance teachers bring to the game."

And yet, Amberry's talent remains mostly untapped. He has privately coached about fifteen students, sometimes for free, and has worked at many high school and college-level basketball clinics. But he admits he's frustrated because no one from the pro ranks has sought him out.

Coach Poteet says that may be because Amberry is too much of an outsider. "They say, 'Here he comes trying to tell us what to do, and he hasn't paid his dues,'" he says. "I guess that's typical in any profession. You think a doctor would accept something that I developed?"

If Amberry were in it for the money, his aim would be laughably low. Ask him about his sponsorships, and he'll tell you he paid full retail for the plastic Hoop Chute that recycles his shots back to the foul line during those lonely morning workouts. Baden, a ball maker, sends him a free ball whenever he asks for it (he wears out about a dozen balls a year). Fila sends him shirts, shoes, and socks. "But by the time you add that up, you're looking at two hundred or three hundred dollars," he says, utterly sincere. "They've been very generous."

Bill Amberry, who at forty-four is the second oldest of Amberry's four sons, says his father's frustration is rooted in his generosity. "When we watch a ball game or go to one and he sees a kid with potential, and in a critical situation this kid doesn't come through and misses a free throw, he's frustrated that he can't help everyone," he says. "Shaq [Lakers center Shaquille O'Neal] time and time again has proven himself a lousy free thrower. My dad is right up that guy's alley. It bothers him that he's got these skills and could help, but they don't seek him out."

Maybe they never will. Maybe Amberry's mastery of his craft came at the wrong time, like the guy who perfected the horse-drawn surrey just as Henry Ford rolled out the first Model T. "I know some people who want to abolish free throws from the game," the older Amberry says. "'They're terrible,' they say. 'They're boring.'"

Amberry shakes his head. He knows as well as anyone that in the television age, style does matter. The rules of pro basketball already have been changed to satisfy the television fan's thirst for action, including the institution of a shot clock to keep things moving.

Those changes may be working. Basketball's fast pace and gravity-defying grace have pushed it past baseball and football in the national consciousness. Basketball culture now drives whole industries, including shoes, clothes, sports drinks, memorabilia, even feature films. Michael Jordan isn't just a basketball star; he's a multimedia deity.

And the seventy-five-year-old podiatrist whose 99.4 percent free throw average is nearly twenty points higher than Jordan's? The phone doesn't ring nearly as often as he'd like. So for now, Tom Amberry has to settle for the satisfaction of chiseling his name, perhaps forever, into the record book. "Free throw shooting is a metaphor for life," he says in a rare moment of philosophical reflection. "They look easy, but they're really difficult. Isn't that how life is?"

POSTSCRIPT

This story is adapted from one that appeared in the May 1998 issue of Orange Coast *magazine. Dr. Tom Amberry continued to practice and shoot almost flawlessly until his mid-eighties, often in charity events, television appearances, and shootouts with NBA greats. He never lost. His final competition was during the 2005 World Masters Games in Edmonton, Alberta, Canada, where he sank all twenty-five of his shots to win the finals against the European free throw champion. He says his talent eventually took him to more than two hundred countries ("All free!"), and the NBA eventually recognized his value to its high-flying brick throwers. He worked for about a year as the free throw coach for the Chicago Bulls. Still, while Amberry had great success coaching high school and college players, his* Make Every Free Throw *coauthor Philip Reed says his impact on pro players was mixed. "When you're dealing with players at that level, it's like going to Phil Mickelson and saying, 'I want to completely overhaul your swing.' Phil's won a lot of tournaments with that swing." Almost until his death at age ninety-four in March 2017, Amberry was still conducting phone consultations with players hoping to improve their free throw percentage, marveling at his late-life basketball success, and getting around his Orange County, California, retirement community on a walker.*

CHAPTER SEVENTEEN

Taking Tinseltown with "The Greatest"

If you thought Parkinson's had knocked out Muhammad Ali, then what's he doing as a late-life Hollywood neophyte at the Four Seasons in Beverly Hills? (1998)

MUHAMMAD ALI EXISTS—HAS ALWAYS EXISTED—IN A MURKY REALM of contradiction, controversy, and peculiar magic. This day at the Four Seasons Hotel in Beverly Hills is no different, but we are focused at the moment on a bright pink silk handkerchief he is holding in his right hand. His mind and eyes are as alive as ever, even though the Parkinson's disease that began eroding his physical abilities in 1981 has dulled the world's most recognizable face and quieted a voice that once enlivened, enraged, and entertained the world. He wants to show me a trick.

Ali loves magic, though his Muslim religion frowns upon it. He does it anyway, mostly to amuse strangers, righting the wrong by later revealing the secrets of his tricks. Nothing makes me happier than seeing through an illusion. So I watch, intent, as Ali curls his fluttering left hand into a fist and begins tucking the handkerchief into the hole between his thumb and index finger. Inch by inch, the pink silk disappears into that storied hand. When it's gone, he gives it a final poke with his right thumb and, with his fist still closed, offers an indecipherable grin.

"Show me," I say.

He opens his empty hand. I touch its talc-smooth palm unselfconsciously, turning it over and looking for an explanation. I know it's a simple magic-store trick. I know the handkerchief has not actually disappeared. And yet, the illusion is perfect. I can't explain what I've just seen, and now I understand his point, wordlessly made.

Nothing with Ali is as it seems.

I approached our meeting in November prepared to chronicle the grim physical and financial slide of a man I once worshipped. I knew about the Parkinson's, knew about the toll the neurological disease has taken on what once was the world's most perfectly tuned body. I also knew that Ali, who turns fifty-six this month, was in the process of selling his eighty-eight-acre farm in Berrien Springs, Michigan, and moving back to his hometown of Louisville, Kentucky. I sensed something foreboding, something distressingly final. Why does a man of his age and uncertain health uproot himself and his family to go home again? Were there money problems? Was he dying?

Another illusion, it turns out. The more startling truth is that Ali is in the midst of what may be his most improbable comeback. He long ago transcended the sport of boxing to become a beloved global symbol of racial and religious pride, but there's one world he never conquered—the world of advertising and commercial endorsement. In his heyday, Ali's image stirred a strange brew of emotions. He was too controversial, too unpredictable, too black, and big-money advertisers looking for a corporate face went elsewhere. But ever since 1996, when the world watched him shaking and alone as he lit the Olympic cauldron in Atlanta, Ali's legend has outgrown even itself. Now, thirty-eight years after he burst into the public consciousness and twenty-seven years after his last professional fight, Muhammad Ali's star is rising once again.

Twice in my professional life, I have found myself talking uncontrollably in the presence of someone I was supposed to be interviewing. The first time was with Fred Rogers, the host of public television's *Mister Rogers' Neighborhood* and perhaps the world's most nonthreatening person. Everything about him—from his unblinking gaze to his cardigan sweater to his deck shoes—screams, "Trust me." Plus, he *listens*. It's utterly disconcerting.

The second time is with Ali. We are in his suite at the Four Seasons, following a photo shoot for a magazine story. Ali, hungry, begins raiding

The aging Muhammad Ali, seemingly comfortable in the body that's betraying him.

the in-room snack cache. As he struggles in silence for several minutes to open a jar of cashews and a box of Earl Grey biscuits, I suddenly begin talking—about the time in 1980 when, as a directionless twenty-three-year-old, I'd made a pilgrimage to his training camp at Deer Lake, Pennsylvania, to watch him prepare for one of his final fights; about the overwhelming emotion of watching him light the Olympic flame, the first time my children ever saw me cry; about the special role he'd played in my life by demonstrating again and again the unshakeable power of personal integrity.

For reasons I still don't understand, I begin showing him photographs of my kids. A soccer picture of my five-year-old son, all uniform and pride and ears. He's just a year younger than the youngest of Ali's nine children, Asaad, and the picture makes him smile. "Girls like him?" Ali asks in a single burst of breath. Then my nine-year-old daughter, with her bright eyes and crooked grin. "Pretty," he says.

Suddenly, I become self-conscious, eager to change the subject. I'm behaving badly, I realize, but why? It's the same impulse I've seen in practically everyone who's drawn into Ali's orbit. Grown men become wide-eyed autograph seekers. Women too young to have known Ali in his prime unselfconsciously hug and kiss the gentle six-foot-two giant when he bends to invite their affection. The impulse to reach out, to touch those hands, to confess your truest feelings, is irresistible.

Perhaps it was always that way, but I imagine it's more so now because the legend exists on a human scale. Ali walks the earth not as a three-time heavyweight champion or a Sixties-era lightning rod of political, racial, and religious emotion, but as a grandfather of two who stumbles occasionally on smooth pavement, who regrets that his children grew up while he was on the road, who brokers deals between Asaad and his babysitting grandmother about whether the six-year-old son can wear short pants in Michigan in November. His wife, Lonnie, keeps hotel room curtains drawn for her husband, whose medication makes his eyes especially sensitive to light. She occasionally helps the nearsighted Ali catch the spots he misses while shaving, and scolds him when she finds Earl Grey biscuit crumbs on the front of his sports shirt.

This is Muhammad Ali today, a mortal beloved, magnetic not just because of who he was, but because of who he is. Ali is a man at peace who seems utterly comfortable in the body that's betraying him. The courage to live openly with his condition—which leaves the mind intact but affects physical coordination and causes tremors—and the rock-solid sense of self he demonstrated throughout his life are why companies such as Apple and a national restaurant chain brought him to Tinseltown to film their new television ad campaigns.

"Ali represents this great combination of incredible talent and presence," says Andy Berndt of TBWA\Chiat\Day in Venice, California, the ad agency that created Apple's ongoing "Think Different" campaign. "He always was who he was, and the world is now looking for people with his courage and passion. I think he's heroic, and he begins to loom larger as time goes on."

"I'd like to see you levitate," I say.

It's another of Ali's favorite illusions. He rises from the couch, the last Earl Grey biscuit in his left hand, and he turns his back to me.

"Watch my feet," he says over his shoulder.

I watch. He's standing in the middle of the floor at a curious angle, his right toe purposefully obscured from my sight. The wait is interminable. His hands are moving, but he's otherwise motionless, touching nothing. The biscuit drops, but he pays it no mind. Then Ali rises, both feet perhaps six inches off the floor. Logically, I know he has balanced, all 250 pounds of him, on the tip of the right toe I cannot see. No small accomplishment, even without Parkinson's. Try it. But for that long and delicious moment, with Muhammad Ali floating like a butterfly, I believe he can do anything.

In the years before the 1996 Summer Games, Ali's wattage had dimmed as he and Lonnie retreated to their tranquil farm along Michigan's St. Joseph River. Don't expect Ali to concede that, of course—"Olympics only made me more famous," he says—but his wife knows the truth. "Americans are enamored with the here and now," she says. "There's Michael Jordan, Charles Barkley, Shaquille O'Neal, Tom Cruise, all these wonderful personalities and beautiful people out there with their smiles and charming faces. But when Muhammad was lighting that torch, standing up there in front of the world with his Parkinson's, it's like we found this jewel that we'd forgotten about. And we took it out and looked at it all over again, and it was still beautiful. The fact is, everybody has an Ali story or an Ali experience, and in that moment he reconnected with all of them."

"Oh my God" was all I could manage when I saw him, and as the image bounced off satellites to every nation on the planet, reactions worldwide were no less visceral. Shortly afterward, longtime Ali friend Howard Bingham says he overheard President Bill Clinton tell Ali that he, too, could not stop his tears.

"Before that happened, we were just going about our lives," Lonnie Ali says. "It was a big secret, so we weren't talking to anybody about it. We were all just caught up in the logistics of him being up there to light that cauldron, but never did he expect the response it got. We just weren't looking for it."

"Ali didn't want to do it," Bingham says. "We had to convince him this was a good thing. He was worried about being embarrassed. When I told him I got a lot of messages that night, and that everybody was crying. He asked, 'Why? They feel sorry for me?' I said no, man, it was just a moment. A hell of a moment."

That moment energized Ali, Lonnie says, as did the ovation he received last March when the documentary film *When We Were Kings* about his dramatic 1974 championship fight with George Foreman won an Academy Award. "The shimmering house of movies stars seemed diminished, their egos preposterous, when Ali rose and stood before them," recalled writer David Maraniss of the *Washington Post* in an article last June. "Yet some saw in that appearance a hint of the maudlin: poor Ali, enfeebled and paunchy, dragged out as yet another melodramatic Hollywood gimmick."

They were wrong. Ali is hardly a sad Joe Louis shuffling around as a Vegas casino greeter. Ali is a man whose mind still has the speed his hands once did and who continues to show the strength of character he showed in risking his career to convert to a controversial and misunderstood religion, and by refusing to step forward when called for the Vietnam-era draft—Ali's proudest moment in a lifetime of unforgettable moments.

By late last spring, interest in Ali for charity events and commercial endorsements had overwhelmed his tight-knit scheduling staff, which includes Lonnie, his two attorneys, Bingham, and Harlan Warner, Ali's primary agent. They needed help. "After the Olympics it just got to be too much," Lonnie says. "And we couldn't handle all the international stuff. We needed to take it to another level."

In June, Ali signed with the International Management Group, the largest sports management and marketing enterprise in the world, which handles athletes such as Tiger Woods, Arnold Palmer, and reigning heavyweight champion Evander Holyfield, alongside whom Ali is pictured in the latest IMG annual report. He is, says Ali's IMG agent Barry Frank, "one of our most saleable clients."

That was not always the case. "You have to remember, in the Sixties and Seventies, you didn't have a lot of blacks endorsing products," Lonnie Ali says. "He did a commercial for a bug killer once. That was a mistake, but it was a good offer and whoever was advising him at the time told him to take it. He did a Toyota commercial once for the Middle East, which makes sense because he's very popular there. But the offers weren't there for a variety of reasons."

For instance, Ali won't endorse products not condoned by his religion, such as pork and alcohol. And social division over his draft resistance persisted long after the Vietnam War ended. Advertisers are always reluctant to risk stirring the wrong emotions. But as with so much else in his life, Ali transcended those things the moment the cameras found him atop the Olympic stadium. "That was the transition from one phase of his life to another," says Frank, who still marvels at the ovations Ali receives during charity dinners and testimonials. "He suddenly became commercially viable."

Although neither Ali nor Frank will talk money figures, Ali's image is prominent in the television, newspaper, and billboard campaign Apple launched in September. The computer company says the campaign "honors creative geniuses who have changed the world," including Ali, Albert

Einstein, Mahatma Gandhi, Thomas Edison, John Lennon, and Pablo Picasso. Apple plans to break a new commercial this month featuring footage of Ali early in his boxing career, jabbing and taunting the camera. He was in Los Angeles in early November to film a commercial for a national food chain that Frank and other IMG officials say focuses on his trademark smile.

"The minute marketing people hear he's available, they say, 'Go get him,'" says IMG's Katie O'Neill, who traveled with the Alis to Los Angeles. "That's the same reaction we're getting from all over the world. It's the emotional tie he seems to have with everyone. Every race. Every age."

"Obviously he has limitations because he can't speak well," says Frank, referring to campaigns that use file footage of Ali rather than newer material. "But he can do things where he's not required to speak." Such as? Frank remains cagey. "Let me just say he's a solid wage-earner at this point."

In a story full of ironies, there's this: Ali couldn't care less.

"He's doing it because it's an easy way to make a living," says his friend Bingham. "He has a family to support and people who depend on him. But he knows he's the most recognizable person on earth. All these things that are happening, he's just not fazed by big times or bright lights."

Ali's focus these days is mostly spiritual. In 1996, Davis Miller wrote a book called *The Tao of Muhammad Ali* describing his personal journey toward becoming a writer, and how it was inspired and fueled by Ali. In it, Miller recalls a conversation the two had in 1989 during which the writer was overwhelmed by the obvious ironies of Ali's disease: "About how he used to talk easier, maybe better, than anybody in the world. About how he sometimes still thinks with speed and dazzle, but it often takes serious effort for him to communicate even with those people close to him. About how he may have been the world's best athlete—when just walking he used to move with the speed and grace of a cat turning a corner. About how it's his left hand, the same hand from which once slid that great Ali snake-lick of a jab, the very hand with which he won more than two hundred thirty fights, it's his *left* hand, not his right, that shakes almost continuously."

It just doesn't seem fair, Miller told him. "I know why this happened," Ali replied then. "God is showing me, and showing you, that I'm just a man, just like everybody else . . . you don't question God."

In the dim suite at the Four Seasons, I ask Ali if he still believes that. The subject of spirituality brightens him. "Everything that happens happens for a reason," he says. "It wouldn't be if it weren't for God. God is the power for me to get into other people's hearts. Allah. You know who Allah is? That's who I work for. Who better? He makes me famous. He makes people love me."

Allah brought him to all these new roles, he says, and I suddenly think of one Ali hasn't even mentioned: as a symbol of hope and courage for people with Parkinson's. My parents have a neighbor name Ted Sandberg. He's a physician—one of the best tippers on my paper route when I was a kid—who now is struggling with Parkinson's. My mother tells me he often wears the Olympic torch pin that the National Parkinson's Foundation adopted as its symbol after 1996. "Before the Olympics, nobody knew what Parkinson's was," Sandberg told me later. "Now everybody's opening up about it."

Janet Reno. Johnny Cash. Billy Graham.

"Million people have Parkinson's," Ali says. He forces the words, but they come stronger and with more emotion, still rhythmic, still poetry. "Hear about people who quit their jobs. Stop going places. Doesn't bother me. Won't stop me from traveling. Won't stop me from doing TV. Just keeps me out of trouble."

Besides, he still has dreams to chase. Lonnie says they're getting too old for Michigan's winters, and they want to move to Louisville to oversee development of a Muhammad Ali museum. Then they plan to move to Las Vegas, to the desert warmth. I ask him if there's anything in life he hasn't done that he still wants to do. "Build a mosque," he says. "The Muhammad Ali Mosque. And a school."

It's an arrangement with God, Lonnie says. In Ali's religion, a mosque builder gets a blessing each time someone prays in his mosque.

Ali wants to get that project rolling, but for now it's unfunded and remains a dream. "He already helped build one in Chicago," Lonnie says. "But he wants to build his own."

I look over at Ali. "Ten thousand people praying," he says, and his eyes are smiling.

It's almost time to go, but not before settling a debt to Allah. From his pocket, Ali pulls a pink silk handkerchief and lays it on the couch. Fastened to one corner is a fake brown thumb. He shows me the trick, tucking the handkerchief completely inside the disembodied digit and slipping the whole thing over his own right thumb. Except for a small ridge at his thumb's first knuckle, the illusion is seamless.

Ali rises, stuffs it back into his pocket, and grabs his aluminum attaché case. The Ali road show must go on, from Los Angeles to Seattle and points beyond, to charity events and meetings and even a huddle with those who are building the official Muhammad Ali website for its April launch. In a week they'll be home, where Asaad, Lonnie's mother, and a much-needed breather await.

But they can't leave just yet. Even though a private limo is idling at the Four Seasons curb to take them to the airport, well-wishers surround Ali the moment he emerges into daylight. The valet parking captain introduces him to the chief of hotel security. A visiting businessman steps forward and drops his British reserve with a thud. "I've always wanted to meet you, Champ," he gushes, grabbing Ali's hand. The crowd grows, eight, ten, twelve, as Lonnie climbs into the car. Ali lingers, basking always in the attention, and he seizes the moment. From his pocket he pulls a sliver of pink silk. The illusion begins again, and nothing is as it seems.

POSTSCRIPT

This essay is adapted from one that originally appeared in the January 1998 issue of Orange Coast *magazine. More than five decades after he burst into the public consciousness as a brash Olympic boxer in 1960, Ali's magic continues into the digital age. As of early 2016, his Facebook page had more than ten million likes, and his @MuhammadAli Twitter handle boasts nearly seven hundred thousand followers. (Wayne Newton, by contrast, has fewer than four thousand.) Ali's popularity did not die when he did in 2016, suggesting that not all legends fade with time.*

CHAPTER EIGHTEEN

Life Begins at 150

Welcome to Nevada's Silver State Open Road Classic, the only car race of its kind in the nation where you can put your feet to the firewall over ninety miles of public road (1993)

ALAN CRITTENDEN, SWATHED HEAD TO TOE IN FIREPROOF CLOTHING, eases his wife's 1992 Corvette toward the starting line. His crash helmet and the dull roar of the car's engine muffle the Garden Grove, California, ironworker's voice, but it's clear enough.

"All right. I'm getting really antsy."

Before him lie ninety miles of what *Motor Trend* magazine calls "the fastest road in America"—two-lane Nevada Highway 318. Behind him are the race director's blunt words about two previous deaths, as well as 105 other drivers who paid to compete in the recent BluBlocker Silver State Open Road Classic.

Beside Crittenden sits his navigator, me, whose idea of living on the edge is having a second bowl of high-fiber cereal. My brain is sending an unmistakable message: Unbuckle that five-point harness, step out of the Corvette's door, and offer the forty-one-year-old Crittenden a hearty "Good luck!" in his quest for 160 miles per hour.

Too late. The starter motions us forward into a cloud of race-fuel fumes exhaled by the hypermodified pickup truck that left twenty seconds before. It's already a pinpoint well down 318. The gregarious and self-confident Crittenden is unusually silent as the starter mouths, "Forty seconds."

Alan Crittenden's Corvette at the Silver State Classic Run starting line
DAVID YODER, THE *ORANGE COUNTY REGISTER*, SEPT. 30, 1993. USED WITH PERMISSION.

My mind wanders. How did Crittenden sleep last night? Is he a generally well-adjusted person? What shared personality trait brought him and dozens of other sports-car buffs to this high-desert place five hours from anywhere? What compels adrenaline junkies, gearheads, and techno-dweebs from all walks of life to live a philosophy best expressed on one spectator's T-shirt: "Wide open 'til ya see God, then brake."

How many seconds did Jim Marcellus of Torrance's Simpson Race Products say this Nomex fire suit would survive a fire? And what was all that prerace talk about sternum-harness decapitations?

A race-course patrol airplane passes overhead, creeping along at only 130 miles per hour. Crittenden, starting fourth, flexes his fingers on the wheel in silence.

"Five, four, three, two, one . . ."

The concept is simple: Find a godforsaken desert road in a state eager to promote tourism, convince authorities to close it to traffic for eight hours, and invite those so inclined to drive it as fast as their gears and guts will allow.

Since the first race in 1988, the twice-yearly Silver State has remained the only foot-to-the-firewall open-road dash in the country. For the most part, this is an orgy of fume-belching, earsplitting muscle cars owned by the people you knew as pistonheads in high school, except now they're grown and have the cash to indulge their obsessions.

Open-road races are among the most challenging in motor sports. Unpredictable turns, blind curves, and hills or uncertain road conditions increase the risk, and there are no guardrails to mitigate mistakes. For that reason, and because of fatal accidents in the 1990 and 1992 races, Silver State Open Road Classic organizers are themselves obsessive—about safety. Technicians carefully inspect each car, requiring additional precautions as the driver's target speed rises. And they don't often compromise.

Santa Ana's Scott Caissie discovered that the hard way. The thirty-two-year-old certified nurse's aide regularly races his 1966 Shelby GT350 at speeds of 145 miles per hour. So he was surprised when Silver State officials approved a top speed of 130 for his car. "I could take my Explorer and do that," he says, walking away in disgust.

Officially, the technicians cited body rust and anchoring problems with the car's roll cage. They also expressed concern about missing bolts, mismounted tires, and wheel bearings that seemed too loose. "I don't play," says the spoilsport tech Tom Roberts of Las Vegas.

Moving into the higher-speed brackets can be expensive. Silver State entry fees rise from $295 for touring-class competitors to $595 for those competing in the unlimited class. Five-point harnesses go for about a hundred bucks each. Roll bars cost about six hundred. Top-rated tires are fifteen hundred dollars a set, and a fireproof outfit—suit, gloves, and a lined helmet—can add an additional thousand to fifteen hundred. The list goes on.

Caissie hustled off to rent a padded safety collar and have his roll cage fixed at an Ely welding shop. His tech speed ultimately was upgraded to 150, and he estimates his car was doing about that when its fan belt fell off three miles into the ninety-mile race. "We probably spent about three thousand dollars getting ready," he says. "They were so rough on everything else, we didn't get around to checking the fan belt."

Race organizer Rodger Ward, a two-time Indianapolis 500 winner from San Bernardino County, says the Silver State "allows people who spend all year doing twenty-right miles per hour in traffic to test their skills, air out their cars, and enjoy the companionship of people like themselves."

It's a diverse group. The list of thirteen registered drivers from Orange County, California, for example, included a commercial airline pilot, a mechanical engineer, an optometrist, a food-equipment salesman, two restaurateurs, and a certified nurse's aide. They joined a field of drivers that included a double amputee, a man who had heart bypass surgery six days earlier, and a last-minute entrant driving a rented Lincoln.

To give everyone a shot at a trophy, the Silver State organizers created various speed brackets ranging from the touring class (top speed: 110 miles per hour) to the unlimited class (where the scent of testosterone is palpable). The goal for racers in all but the unlimited class is to complete the race with an average speed as close as possible to their target speed.

To my chagrin, Crittenden is competing in the unlimited class, meaning that he wants to drive the course as fast as he can. The only consolation is that the race technicians have limited his Corvette to a top speed of 160 mph based on its performance ability and safety equipment.

In contrast to the sophisticated split-time charts, stopwatches, and laptop computers employed by some other competitors, Crittenden's race strategy is crude: "If you hear the tires squealing in the Narrows (a winding section of 318 that is every racer's biggest challenge), then we're about right."

But Crittenden has a secondary strategy. With only six cars entered in the unlimited class, and with the tendency of those often-exotic cars to break down, he hoped a mid-150-mph average would be fast enough to place him among the fastest finishers in that category. Maybe, just maybe, a regular guy in a regular Corvette could find a back door into the winner's circle of the race's most prestigious speed class.

That attitude represents what Mission Viejo's Brady Gross describes as the essence of the Silver State race. "The typical driver is a car enthusiast who isn't out there for their image," says the thirty-one-year-old owner of a stitching business, Embroidery Advantage in Tustin, which supports the black 1990 Corvette ZR-1 he considers a hobby. "Sure, there are a lot of image cars like Ferraris and such. But everyone is driving it because they like performance, not because they want to be seen. There aren't a lot of posers."

Crittenden says the race is an opportunity to get the need for speed out of his system, "the poor man's chance to go fast legally. I just like driving, and have since high school. And I had a lot of speeding tickets when I was younger. I look at it this way: The price I pay [to enter the race] is about what I'd pay in citations. And this is safer."

The digital speedometer of Crittenden's aquamarine Corvette climbs faster than the numbers on a super-premium gas pump. Never mind that it's basically a stock model, a Christmas 1991 present to his wife, Terri, that he modified only with a roll bar, a high-intake air cleaner, and a muffler system that allows it to breathe easier in this high-desert area's six-thousand-foot elevation. The car hurtles into triple digits without shudder or sweat.

I, on the other hand, have borrowed a technique from childbirth class. The seams of my fireproof suit become my focal point.

Through the wire snaking from a small tape recorder into Crittenden's helmet, the driver hears his wife reading detailed course notes based on a theoretical 150-mph run. That low-tech answer to the timing and navigation systems employed by more exacting racers frees me to concentrate fully on my anxieties. As desert real estate begins to smear past the windows, I sink my fingernails into the thin illusion of journalistic immunity and wonder again what sort of people would do this.

Somewhere behind him, Marjorie and Pete Ricci of Huntington Beach are preparing to launch their 1965 Mustang. They began restoring the car for their daughter and got carried away. "It turned out to be a from-the-ground-up conversion for this race," says Marjorie, the driver. Her husband, a senior engineer at McDonnell Douglas, heard about the Silver State from coworker Karen Smith of Los Alamitos, who at the moment is strapping into a 1970 Mustang navigated by her husband,

Gary. (Karen Smith's advice to navigators: "You can whimper, but you can't scream.")

Rick and Michele Doria of Huntington Beach, who own the Haus of Pizza in Costa Mesa, compete individually. The thirty-nine-year-old Rick starts two cars ahead of Crittenden in his no-nonsense black 1985 Corvette; Michele is waiting behind him in her white 1986 Corvette decorated with red chili pepper decals.

"We work hard, so when we have a chance to play, we play hard," says the twenty-eight-year-old Michele, whose mother, Bonnie Mullen of Tucson, is navigating for her daughter for a second time. "I work seventy hours a week in a mom-and-pop joint that's as busy as heck. When we're not there, we really need something different. You can't just go home and do your gardening."

Anaheim optometrist Paul Habener, saying "there's a little Walter Mitty in us all," applies Zen-like terms to the Silver State experience: "It's a wonderful feeling going one hundred forty miles per hour. At those speeds, you feel a oneness with your vehicle. You're tied to it like a fetus to its mother."

This particular mother just hit 140. I follow along on my backup course notes, supplementing Terri Crittenden's recording with hand signals. Right turn at odometer reading 3.54. Down hill. Up hill. Decelerate in, accelerate out. Crittenden, competing in his fourth Silver State race, drives the turns with infectious confidence, often positioning the car a mile or more in advance to drive the best line.

The road itself offers unexpected solace. Through the wavering heat, I can see most of 318's bends and turns long before we reach them. And the immediate reality, the car's interior, is so familiar that the exterior reality seems less frightening. On the first five-and-a-half-mile straightaway, Crittenden breaks through the psychological and technical barrier acknowledged by other drivers and the slogan "Life begins at 150."

That's when the tires near their limit. The car gets finicky. Road bumps imperceptible at legal speeds become bone-jarring threats that can launch the car airborne. This, after all, is ninety miles of public road, not some manicured racetrack. How had Habener, the Anaheim optometrist, put it? "When you get over one-fifty, that's where problems are going to happen. Above one-sixty, the stress factors on your car are cubed root. If something happens, you don't have time to do anything."

Who's Crittenden waving to? Drivers shouldn't be waving at 160 miles per hour. But somewhere along 318, his friend, course worker Don Raines of Anaheim, waves back.

The speed, if not comfortable, is at least becoming familiar. Hints of danger pass too quickly for comprehension. A deer-crossing sign. Some form of local wildlife reduced to a pulpy pile on the centerline. Crittenden opens and closes his hands on the steering wheel, a relaxation technique employed by many drivers. The Corvette flashes past the first starter, a purple Porsche. It's parked well off the road, broken down. Same with the third vehicle, the pickup truck that started just ahead of Crittenden. Some miles beyond that, a shredded tire tread. Might the second starter, Huntington Beach's Rick Doria, be out as well?

"We may be the first car to finish," I shout.

But Crittenden knows what's ahead. Was that a yellow forty-five mph sign with a squiggling arrow?

The speedometer reads 130 as Crittenden enters the Narrows, a seven-curve canyon with very large, very dense boulders littering the road shoulder. He'd dreamed about the Narrows the night before. The gauge briefly dips to 111 as the car hits the apex of a particularly sharp left, but otherwise stays between 120 and 130. The Corvette roars out of the canyon and Crittenden heads for the finish line a little more than seventeen mostly straight miles away. I exhale.

A small but enthusiastic crowd is waiting about a mile south of the finish line. Rick Doria and his navigator are there; the shredded tire becomes a mystery. There's a smattering of race officials and cooperative law enforcement officers.

Crittenden pulls the car onto the shoulder, parks, and pulls the helmet from his damp head. For the first time, I notice that wrapping oneself in fireproof Nomex and driving through the desert with the air conditioning off is a very hot thing to do. As I shake Crittenden's hand,

I'm surprised at my reaction—disappointment that the ride was over so soon. We'd covered ninety miles in thirty-five minutes and twenty-four seconds.

Other racers arrive at regular intervals. A smiling Gross reports hitting 170 and pronounces it "very enjoyable." The purple Porsche broke down just as Doria was about to pass, and he notes matter-of-factly that "we went past him at one-sixty-five."

Mission Viejo's twenty-seven-year-old Matt Shelor navigated for his dad, Darrell, of Anaheim, an American airlines pilot. "Whoooeee!" he says, climbing from their Nissan 300 ZX. "That's not something you do every day!"

Later than night, when the racers gather for the awards banquet at a Las Vegas hotel, Crittenden, the regular guy in the regular Corvette, gets good news: His average speed of 152.5424 mph, along with his back-door strategy, was enough for third place in the unlimited category. He got an engraved trophy. For my role as quivering ballast, I got a navigator's trophy: an engraved Lucite clipboard.

Says the overly generous Crittenden: "I guess we just outdrove them."

POSTSCRIPT

This essay is adapted from a story originally in the September 30, 1993, issue of the Orange County Register. *The visionary and organizer of what's now called the Silver State Classic Challenge, two-time Indy 500 champ Rodger Ward, died in July 2004, but the race has continued and evolved since its early days. By 2003 it had two certificates from Guinness World Records, including "Fastest Road Race" and "Highest Speed on a Public Highway." In 2012, competitor Jim Peruto, driving a modified 2006 Dodge Charger, set a new record during which his average speed over the 90-mile course was 217.557 miles per hour. A few days later, according to the event's website, the Nevada Department of Transportation voted to rename Highway 318 as "The Silver State Classic Challenge Highway."*

CHAPTER NINETEEN

The Toilet-Valve Titan

Sitting down with the Southern Californian who changed the way we flush, on the eve of his induction into the national Plumbing Industry Hall of Fame (1989)

AMONG GERMANY'S WORLD WAR II REFUGEES WHO MADE THEIR WAY into the bright southwest corner of California in the late 1930s, Adolf Schoepe sits alone. And please forgive the pun, because at Fluidmaster Inc., among men comfortable with the phrases "carry power" and "gallons per flush," all conversations begin and end at the same place—the toilet.

This is inevitable. The cornerstone of the Fluidmaster empire is an unconventional, do-it-yourself toilet tank valve that will account for 90 percent of the Anaheim company's projected forty million dollars in sales this year. Toilets are his life, admits company founder Schoepe (sadly pronounced *sho-pee*), and the evidence is everywhere at corporate headquarters on Via Burton Street. Notes an otherwise dignified corporate publication: "Fluidmaster people have an entirely different relationship with toilets."

The eve of Schoepe's induction into the national Plumbing Industry Hall of Fame seemed an appropriate time to tour one of Orange County's most successful and good-humored small businesses; to see the Fluidmaster lab with its twelve toilets and ten eternally flushing test chambers; to trace the evolution of Schoepe's valve in the company's shrine-like display; and, indeed, to meet the energetic eighty-five-year-old man who this week will see his name enshrined alongside those of R. T. Crane, Walter Kohler, and forty-five other plumbing legends.

"Schoepe really is one of the really big success stories in the plumbing industry," says Charles C. Horton, whose Skokie, Illinois, company publishes *Supply House Times*, the nation's leading plumbing magazine in which eight new Hall of Fame honorees will be named later this week. "You don't have to be big to be good."

The man who is changing the way we flush still works long days in a book-lined, second-floor office in the elegant, mirrored-glass Fluidmaster headquarters. He retains a slight German accent more than sixty years after emigrating, but the official portrait of Ronald Reagan and framed birthday wishes from the former president Schoepe keeps on display underscore his loyalty to the country where he found, as Fluidmaster's thirtieth anniversary brochure says, "success and fulfillment of the ultimate American dream."

First, some history. The Fluidmaster story begins, according to the brochure, with Schoepe's birth in a small German town, which at the time had no running water. In chapters headlined "The Early Years," "The Beginning," and "Decade of Growth," the brochure traces Schoepe's rise from dead-broke immigrant metal craftsman to his successful founding of the Kwikset lock company. But the focus of Schoepe's life shifted from door locks to toilets in the mid-1950s when an inventor named Kit Doyle showed Schoepe a "revolutionary" new valve that defied generations of toilet dogma and, Schoepe thought, could forever alter the mysterious inner workings of the nation's tank-type commodes.

In short, Doyle's valve worked on the logical principle that it's easier to work *with* water pressure than *against* it. Instead of relying on a conventional rod-and-float-ball system, in which the ball is forced *up* by rising water until there's enough leverage to force *down* a shut-off switch at the other end of the rod, Doyle's valve simply floated a ball up a plastic shaft until it tripped a shut-off switch.

Although the mostly plastic valve was more expensive than the conventional type—the best model today sells for between four and nine dollars retail—it easily could be installed by homeowners who once might have paid a plumber handsomely to correct the leaks, whistles, and other maladies common in conventional valves. They're so easy to install that even a bumbling plumbing neophyte like me once successfully installed three Fluidmaster valves in a single afternoon.

Schoepe, who now spends one day a week at his nine-hundred-acre citrus ranch in San Diego County, decided to stake his future on the do-it-yourself valve, a decision corporate literature says was fraught with "grave doubts." When Kwikset merged with American Hardware Corp., which was reluctant to diversify into plumbing, Schoepe bought Doyle's design, formed Fluidmaster in 1957, and set about fine-tuning the valve that a recent *Domestic Engineering* magazine survey said is now preferred two-to-one by plumbing contractors.

"I was in a fortunate position," Schoepe says of the eighteen months it took to get his valve to market. "I had built up enough resources at Kwikset and was able to survive the difficult times a new business always has."

Plumbing revolutionary Adolf Schoepe in the toilet museum at Fluidmaster, 1989
PHOTO BY JEBB HARRIS, THE *ORANGE COUNTY REGISTER*. USED WITH PERMISSION.

Today, as senior vice president Fred Schmuck leads a tour of Fluidmaster's headquarters and production facilities, it's obvious that Schoepe's gamble paid off.

Schmuck is a master salesman, and Schoepe credits him with helping overcome plumbing industry prejudice against Fluidmaster's strange new valve. He leads me first into the hallway that serves as a sort of toilet-valve museum. He gestures toward the original prototype of the Model 400, mounted like a jewel on a hardwood base beneath a Plexiglas dome, and then to the subsequent—and similarly mounted—incarnations of Fluidmaster's valve.

Schmuck lingers briefly, silently, over the display before pushing on into the manufacturing area. He opens a door to a shop where an estimated ten million dollars in whirring, custom-designed valve-making machines are busy spitting out the estimated forty thousand toilet valves Fluidmaster will produce this day. Each one will be hand-tested and hung on an overhead conveyor, from which the valves dangle until ready for automated packaging.

"We'll make nine million this year," Schmuck says, and that number becomes downright startling when you consider that there are only about two hundred million toilets in the United States. (You can read about such things in Fluidmaster's two staff-produced publications, "News Leak" and "Think Tank.")

Schmuck moves on into the lab, where someone has mounted several toilet-related commemoratives, including a poster of historically significant toilets ("The Sultan With Decoration, 1896"), the patent claim for "Crapper's Valveless Water Waste Preventer," and the dignified black-and-white portrait of Sir Thomas Crapper, inventor of the flush toilet.

"We save that as a living tribute," Schmuck says, noting that the photo is draped in black once a year when the company observes the anniversary of Crapper's death with a twenty-one-flush salute.

Several of the dozen test toilets are running, but their sound is overwhelmed by that of the ten toilet-valve test chambers. Inside each chamber, a Fluidmaster valve is being put through its paces. Some gurgle and flush at a frantic pace; others empty and refill at a more leisurely rate. The regimen continues day and night, a high-speed simulation of the heroic valve's life in the field.

The tour over all too soon, Schmuck leads me from the lab into the engineering department, where dramatic, computer-generated diagrams of the famous valve are mounted, matted like art prints, framed in chrome, and hung on the walls. As we move away from the lab, we leave behind the sound of ceaseless flushing—perhaps the finest imaginable salute to the man who started a peculiar plumbing revolution.

POSTSCRIPT

This essay is adapted from a story that first appeared in the July 3, 1989, issue of the Orange County Register. *Adolf Schoepe remained active at Fluidmaster well into his nineties, and according to his obituary in the* Los Angeles Times, *he served as chairman until his death in 2001 at the age of 97. According to Bob Connell, then a Fluidmaster executive vice president, Schoepe often "was down on the floor every day, talking to employees and personally inspecting parts." The company he founded remains family owned and operated, with Schoepe's son, Robert Anderson Schoepe, at the helm, and today has offices and manufacturing plants in Mexico, China, Turkey, the UK, and Slovenia. With a distribution network across more than eighty countries, it sells more toilet tank replacement valves than any other manufacturer in the world, and its product line now includes dual flush valves, flappers, tank levers, toilet repair kits, connectors, and something called "bowl wax."*

CHAPTER TWENTY

Corky Ra's Peculiar Master Plan

When hairless blue-toned humanoids tell you to move from Orange County, California, to Utah, build a pyramid, and mummify your cat, you don't ask a lot of questions (1986)

SUMMUM BONUM AMEN RA—"CORKY" TO HIS FRIENDS—WAS MEDItating on the couch in his girlfriend's apartment when it began. He was listening to his internal vibrations, "the ringing in your ears, except it's inside your head," when the sound suddenly became very intense.

"The next thing I knew I was standing in front of an enormous pyramid," he says. "I walked around to one side and saw an oval building that looked like it was made of black graphite. I walked right through the wall and there were these individuals inside. They were silently communicating with me."

What the "evolved souls" were telling him, he says, were the answers to mankind's persistent questions about the meaning of life. He remembers his teachers were hairless, blue-toned humanoids familiar with the natural laws described in ancient Egyptian texts. Through a crystal that rose through the floor, he says they imparted the wisdom that would become the foundation of the religion he founded following the experience, and the blueprint for a life spent in pursuit of some astonishing goals.

"I felt like I was being programmed. I was being loaded with information," says the 1962 graduate of Tustin High School in central Orange County, California. "I saw then that all this was going to happen."

As he speaks, he's sitting in his thirty-eight-foot-high pyramid in Salt Lake City, Utah, flanked by an altar laden with large quartz crystals, a fifteen-hundred-gallon vat of fermenting wine, and his mummified cat. "There was a real trauma about whether I was going crazy or not, and I was very apprehensive about telling anyone about this."

No more. Today, Amen Ra gladly talks about his mission and the increasingly ambitious projects upon which he has embarked since that experience in 1975. His initial goal was to build the pyramid and establish a winery, no simple task in the suspicious, Mormon-controlled state of Utah. His new religion demanded meditational "nectars" made in a pyramid where the energy resonance is just right. Based upon his plea for religious need, the Utah Liquor Control Commission awarded him license No. 001 in 1981. Amen Ra's remains the only licensed winery in the state.

More recently, Amen Ra has been trying to introduce Egyptian-style mummification as a burial option in the US funeral industry, a proposal that government and industry officials aren't quite sure how to handle. "I don't know that mummification is a term defined by California law," says James Allen, executive director for the state Board of Funeral Directors and Embalmers.

In July, *People* magazine anointed Amen Ra a "would-be mummy mogul"—"would be" because none of the fifty people he says have signed contracts for the service have died yet. The story proclaimed, "mummification has put Summum on the map," but mentioned only briefly that Amen Ra's most notable mummification to date is that of his cat, Oscar, who in the spring died in his arms of feline leukemia.

Taken out of context, Amen Ra's schemes might suggest a certain eccentricity on the part of one of Southern California's more innovative entrepreneurs. Actually, the full story of Amen Ra's strange journey from Orange County to Salt Lake City, and eventually back again, doesn't help much either.

Characteristically buoyant, Amen Ra was in Southern California late last month scouting potential sites for an even more ambitious project than national neo-mummification. He wants to build a giant pyramid complex

Summum Bonum Amen Ra at his Salt Lake City pyramid, 1986
PHOTO BY TODD BUCHANAN, THE *ORANGE COUNTY REGISTER*, NOV. 10, 1986. USED WITH PER-
MISSION.

here, and although he hasn't worked out the specifics yet, he was trying to find space for the facility in the master plan of the Irvine Company, which is in the process of developing the ninety-three-thousand-acre Irvine Ranch—covering much of the sunny paradise better known as Orange County—into what many consider the finest example of master planning in the country.

Never mind that the master plan to date overlooked the need for a spiritually based pyramid complex amid its meticulously designed suburban residential and retail communities. Amen Ra chose Orange County because "the people who live here have great consciousness." He says he'd prefer something on top of a hill with an ocean view, revealing a charming naïveté about the essential nature of the multibillion-dollar land development company into whose master plan he was trying to insert himself.

Again, no matter. The complex—which he expects to take years and as much as twenty-six million dollars to complete—is intended to serve mankind on two levels: the physical and the metaphysical. First, it would include a funeral home, a hospice, and a childbirth facility to ease entry and exit from this life. Second, it ideally would include a twenty-story pyramid through which Amen Ra and Summum members could focus the collective energy of Southern Californians and cause a series of small earthquakes that would ease the stress on the area's geologic plate system. Amen Ra believes the smaller quakes will prevent a larger, more devastating earthquake.

Certain that financial support will be forthcoming—the same kind of "possibility thinking" that drew the Rev. Robert Schuller of the Crystal Cathedral and other spiritual leaders to increasingly affluent Orange County—Amen Ra has established a "Catastrophic Earthquake Prevention Trust" account at an Irvine bank. Although advertising is not set to begin for another month, Summum member Ron Zefferer of Santa Ana says several hundred dollars already have trickled in.

"I don't say maybe it won't get built, because I really do believe it will get built," Zefferer says. "I'll allow for the fact that sometimes things don't happen, but I know we're going to build a pyramid down there of significant size. I can't say it's going to be built by April 5, 1989, but I'm sure within the next five to seven years we'll have the ground to put it on and it will be under construction."

Amen Ra didn't tell Larry Heglar, the director of land sales at the Irvine Company, exactly what he had in mind when they met October 29. "I didn't want to freak the guy out in the first conversation. I just wanted to see what was available."

Heglar told him there might be some acreage on a distant ridge near the north border of Laguna Beach, and told him it would be very expensive. "He didn't say money was no object," Heglar says, "but it didn't seem to make any difference to him."

Although there are allowances for churches in the company's master plan, Heglar says planners would consider the degree to which a given church is represented in the community and would be very selective about the types of structures they allow. "I told him I didn't think it was impossible," Heglar says, "but I said I couldn't be very optimistic."

Confidence comes naturally to Amen Ra, and in the eleven years since his metaphysical transformation, he has built Summum from a one-man vision into a nonprofit charitable organization in which about two hundred active members—his estimate—dedicate themselves to the somewhat nebulous goal of trying to "understand the underlying forces of nature." Through it all, the Summum founder says he has refused to be swayed from the agenda imparted by the evolved souls.

Amen Ra's offbeat theology led a curious Kern County mortician, John Sams, to Salt Lake City, where in March Sams discussed mummification with the group. He left after concluding that Summum is "another offshoot of some California cult."

That many regard Amen Ra as an excellent candidate for a straitjacket is not surprising given that, for a five-dollar donation meant to help fund the Orange County pyramid project, he will furnish a stack of affidavits signed by witnesses to his "miracles" and notarized by a Summum member. They attest to Amen Ra's responsibility for at least one immaculate conception, the telepathic sealing of a power-steering fluid leak, mental orgasms triggered by bell ringing, the apparent telepathic repair of a broken telephone, and "unusually prolonged exhaling." Summum members also ascribe to Amen Ra the ability to light candles with his fingertips, heal the sick, pour wine from a bottle that always remains full, and create rain, thunder, lightning, wind, and earthquakes.

"Sometimes you have to touch people in a different way," Amen Ra says when asked about the miracles. "It's a gift given to me—and it's certainly not exclusive—to allow the life force within me to touch the life force within them. I communicate and they interpret what the words are to be."

And what about the skeptics? From behind a beard as thick and well-trimmed as carpet, Amen Ra smiles: "They said the same thing ten years ago when we told them we had to have a winery in Salt Lake City."

It's the same smile evident on a clean-shaven Corky King in his high school yearbook photo. But looking back on it now, steering his six-year-old Toyota from the small tomato farm where Summum grows food for

Salt Lake City's poor toward his daily aerobics class, Amen Ra admits that there was nothing particularly reassuring about his life to that point.

"I wasn't too metaphysical back then," he says. "Maybe I was. I don't know."

Born in Salt Lake City forty-two years ago, Amen Ra began life with the name Claude Nowell. His parents divorced when he was five, and his mother, Grace, moved him and his two sisters to Monrovia, in the San Gabriel Valley foothills of Los Angeles County. In 1952, she married Robert Williamson King. The family moved to Tustin in 1958 and young Corky eventually enrolled in Tustin High School. He worked for his father's homebuilding firm in Salt Lake City during the summers. After graduating from high school in 1962 and taking community college classes, he decided to move to Utah and work for his dad full time.

His father, a Mormon in name if not practice, insisted his son get involved in the church. After undertaking a yearlong mission, he began studying business at Brigham Young University. He later transferred to the University of Utah, where records indicate he never completed work for any degree, although he was enrolled in a master's degree program. He married in 1970 and had two children during his four-year marriage. During that time, while working as an administrative manager for a welding equipment supply distributor and later for a Salt Lake City printing company, Corky King began his search for the meaning of life.

The search ended during his 1975 meeting with the evolved souls, he says. He formed Summum, legally changed his name from Corky King to Summum Bonum Amen Ra, and set about building a religion that seems drawn from equal parts Egyptian theology, meditation psychology, and pop cosmology. The founder defines Summum as "the totality of all that is," so its tenets also include trace elements of Hinduism, Christianity, Judaism, and other established religions.

Today, Amen Ra lives in the shadow of a steel-fabricating plant in a heavy industrial section of Salt Lake City, on a one-third-acre lot across the street from a freeway. His property contains a pleasant frame home, seven peacocks, two large dogs, a hand-painted iron gate that reads "Summum," and two shingled pyramids, the larger of which doubles as Summum's spiritual headquarters, and the winery, where he says the group makes "the worst-tasting wine in the world" based upon formulas he says were drawn from the Bible, the Egyptian Book of the Dead, and the Tibetan Book of the Dead.

Members sometimes travel from as far away as Orange County and Arizona for the Sunday meetings in the pyramid. Videotapes of those gatherings, available to members who cannot attend, show members seated on couches around a white-robed Amen Ra. Members sip Summum-made "nectar" and talk about death, their fear of dying, and mummification, a process that members believe is the gentlest way to move between the physical and spiritual worlds. They gather in front of a makeshift altar littered with what Amen Ra considers religiously significant bric-a-brac. There are carefully arranged quartz crystals, which according to Indian texts described in a Summum handout, vibrate with the natural frequency of the universe. Inside a tiny brass jewel box is a dead scarab brought from Egypt. Amen Ra says the beetle symbolizes the transformation of the soul from this world into the next.

The altar decorations offer only one hint that Summum has a commercial as well as a spiritual purpose. On a nearby shelf sits Oscar, Amen Ra's dead cat, who has no particular religious significance but who passed on in the spring just as Summum was gearing up its push for commercial mummification. In a sense, Oscar—gold-leafed and poised for eternity— is Summum's floor model.

For the first ten years of its existence, Summum members dealt with death and mummification in abstract terms. It wasn't until attorney Michael J. Burdell, a core Summum member, was killed by an escaped prisoner during a courthouse shootout in Salt Lake City last year that Amen Ra began looking for someone to develop a mummification process. The search for technology to provide "permanent body preservation" didn't take him far.

Kerry Peterson, a mortician-science assistant at the nearby University of Utah, always had been intrigued by Egyptian burial practices and had developed a process he thought improved upon the traditional methods. He liked the historical possibilities that mummification presented. Instead of future archaeologists sifting through broken pieces of bone and skull fragments to gain some insight into twentieth-century man, Peterson says, "there will be a very detailed picture of what people were like here."

Peterson also was fascinated by the possibility that an individual's genetic codes might be lifted from mummified tissue—as was done recently by a Swedish scientist working with a 2,400-year-old Egyptian mummy—and when technology permits, cloned. So when Amen Ra called him and asked if such a mummification process was possible, he said it was and allowed Summum to file a patent application for the process.

It's not pretty. First, the body is drained and refilled with an embalming solution enriched with extra preservatives, mold retardants, and chemicals that keep the tissues moist. The internal organs are removed, and the body and organs are submerged for two weeks in a tank filled with preservative solution. The tank allows oxygen to escape but not enter, removing as much oxygen as possible from the body. After the soaking, the body is removed from the tank, the body cavities are stuffed with an absorbent filler and sewn shut. The organs are placed in canopic jars filled with preservative solution and welded shut.

The body then is wrapped in treated linen, covered with material similar to that used in surgical gloves, and wrapped again in linen. Over that layer, the body is sealed in a substance similar to plaster of paris and finally placed in a mummiform, which also is welded shut. The air is removed through tiny holes at either end and replaced with argon, an inert gas, and the holes are sealed.

Alas, Peterson's union with Amen Ra came too late for Burdell. The slain Summum member was cremated and his ashes sealed in a custom-made stainless steel pyramid, which during a recent visit to Summum headquarters was sitting atop a shower in the bottling house.

The US funeral industry has undergone a revolution in the past decade, rocked by the public's growing acceptance of cremation as an inexpensive option to more elaborate burial services. Summum offers yet another alternative. When its services are requested, it will dispatch the necessary equipment to any of the fifty states, along with "licensed mummification specialists"—though it's not exactly clear who does the licensing. Summum offers mummification at prices ranging from $7,500 to $500,000, with the cost depending mostly upon the type of mummiform chosen. The King Tut–style one that Summum members have been hauling around to funeral industry trade shows is a mid-range model.

Summum's specialists will advise the local mortician about how to proceed with the mummification. As long as it's handled by an embalmer licensed by the state in which the work is done, Summum is doing nothing illegal. Once the body is prepared, Summum considers the spiritual disposition of the soul a matter of individual discretion—unless, of course, the deceased asks in advance to be led through the seventy-seven-day Egyptian process of "transference," which Summum will provide in a Summum-designated pyramid.

Because of the expense, though, enthusiasm for Summum's service among the area funeral directors is somewhat muted. "Out of two hundred forty million registered birth certificates, there have to be one tenth of one percent out there who are clutching for something new, unique, and different, whether it's having your remains rocketed into orbit or scattered at sea," Kern County mortician Sams says. "They'll find someone out there to whom this appeals."

Julie Garvin, a fifty-one-year-old set and costume designer, is considering a seven-dollar-a-month prepayment plan offered by Summum. "I never have wanted to be buried," she says. "I always thought I would be cremated, and in fact had determined that was what I was going to do." An active metaphysicist for thirty years but not a Summum member, Garvin changed her mind and signed up for mummification after attending a lecture by Summum member Zefferer.

Amen Ra says it's that type of open-mindedness that drew him to affluent Orange County as he began raising funds for the Catastrophic Earthquake Prevention Trust, and he hopes that openness to new ideas will make the pyramid complex project a success. While buzzing along the Pacific Coast Highway two weeks ago in a borrowed subcompact, he occasionally veered onto the shoulder, stopped, and pointed out ocean-view hilltops between Corona del Mar and Laguna Beach that might serve Summum's purposes. "Any one of those ridges would be ideal for us," he says, but by then the Irvine Company had made clear that a giant, quasi-religious pyramid didn't really fit into its master plan.

Arriving at the northern border of Laguna Beach, Amen Ra pulled over again. From there he could see the hilltop ridge the company's Heglar had described as possibly available. It was pleasant enough, but there was an obvious problem: The site was crossed by power lines. "We want to avoid those," Amen Ra says. "The electromagnetic field around them interferes with the pyramidal environmental state."

As he drove back along MacArthur Boulevard, past high-rises and commercial clutter near John Wayne Airport, he marveled at the area's growth since the days he spent cruising that stretch of road. "Look at what's happened here in twenty years," he says. "This used to be all bean fields and orange groves. If this can happen, maybe we *will* have our pyramid down here on the coast."

By late afternoon, Amen Ra was on a plane to Salt Lake City. It had been a quick two-day trip, but he needed to get back. There was much to be done.

POSTSCRIPT

This essay is adapted from a story that appeared in the November 10, 1986, edition of the Orange County Register. *To date, no Summum-backed twenty-story pyramid complex stands on a hilltop along the Orange County, California, coast, or anywhere else. The American funeral industry has not seen a significant rise in the number of people requesting mummification as a burial option. However, Summum Bonum Amen Ra apparently did return to Southern California, and a few years after this story appeared, I spotted him teaching aerobics classes at Racquetball World in Santa Ana. His students knew him as Corky. Alas, according to Summum's website, he died in January 2008 at age 63, and became the first human to be mummified by the group he founded.*

CHAPTER TWENTY-ONE

Toenail Polish for Fluffy

The peculiar social pathology displayed floor to ceiling inside one of the country's largest pet supplies warehouses (1988)

DICK FREEMAN PLUCKS AN ODDLY SHAPED CERAMIC OBJECT FROM A towering shelf in one of the country's largest pet supplies warehouses. In the middle of a tour in which he points out no less than three different colors of toenail polish for dogs, Freeman deadpans a joke that's remarkably convincing.

"These are dog urinals," he says, holding the small, open-faced basin that, sure enough, would make a believable target for a deadeye dog. But he can't contain his smile. "No, no, don't write that. Actually, it's a bird dish."

Pardon his giddiness. ASU, the Anaheim, California, company for which he is marketing director, is experiencing a level of success more often the stuff of dreams. The pet products distributor, which deals only with specialty pet stores, expects more than thirty million dollars in sales from a product line that includes squeaky latex turkey legs, electronic flea collars, and "natural" rawhide cocktail franks.

Since its founding by current president Keith Bonner in 1973, ASU has grown from a 2,400-square-foot aquarium supply house into a 110,000-square-foot giant in an industry that last year generated more than two billion dollars in retail pet-store sales. Its product inventory swelled from seven hundred to ten thousand items, and its growth has been so rapid that the company had to expand its facilities seven times in the past fifteen years.

While ASU is among the largest pet products distributors in the nation, it certainly isn't the only one making money. At 30 percent a year, its growth is just slightly better than that of the entire pet industry, which according to a 1987 survey by *Pet Dealer Magazine*, was up 24 percent, or $420 million, from 1986.

The implications are more interesting than the sales figures. Some industry analysts and social psychologists regard the boom as a window into the American psyche. What buried need is revealed by the current demand for a safe, comfortable car seat for dogs? What lifestyle changes are fueling the unprecedented popularity of high-rise, lushly carpeted "cat condos"? What pathological urge are manufacturers exploiting with their lines of pet cologne and "color enhancer [that] brightens dull and lusterless dog coats"?

"The greatness of a nation and its moral progress can be judged by the way its animals are treated," wrote Mohandas K. Gandhi, but what might the mahatma have made of the black-and-gold argyle dog sweater that Freeman now is removing from its plastic wrap? Or of ASU's humming Digital VAX 11/750 computer that helps speed box loads of squeaky latex Smurfs, "Sporty Mice" catnip toys, and boxes of four tiny rain galoshes to pet stores all over California and Arizona?

"There really seems to have been a burgeoning of the upscale end of the pet-products market," says Steven T. King, a spokesman for the Washington, DC–based Pet Industry Joint Advisory Council. "Everything from expensive aquariums that look like fancy furniture to expensive items for your dog. Pet boutiques are growing up in the major urban areas to cater to the yuppie buyer who wants that extra special crystal dog bowl or fur coat for their pet."

Theories afoot relate the boom to the dissolution of the traditional family and the documented calming effects pets have on their owners, but those theories explain only part of the shift that has seen pets become less "like" a member of the family and more a family member with a recognized—and highly valued—role. What's more, the same social-label

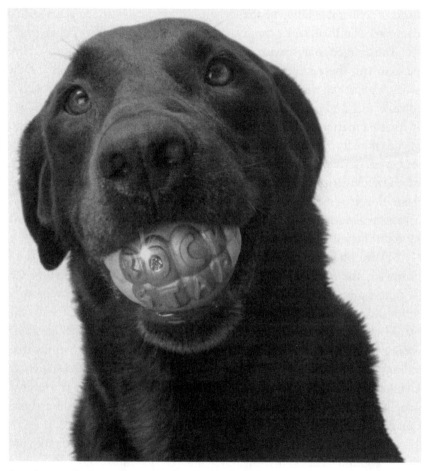

Are changes in the traditional American family behind the pet products boom?
PHOTO COURTESY OF MOODY PET INC. OF PHILADELPHIA, PENNSYLVANIA

sensitivity that turned garbage collectors into "sanitation engineers" and secretaries into "executive assistants" has turned the pets of the late 1980s into "companion animals."

"People are becoming more aware of the important roles animals play in their lives," says Linda Hines, executive director of the Delta Society, an international nonprofit professional organization that focuses on the interactions of people, animals, and the environment. "People today make a deliberate choice to share their life for maybe fifteen years with a companion animal, and I think that attitude is part of what's changing."

The burgeoning service industry for the nation's pets may have peaked with the establishment of Canine Cryobank Inc. of Pacific Palisades, California, which since 1981 has engaged in the lucrative practice of collecting and freezing dog semen. (And never mind how they collect it. That's a matter best left private between the donor, a "teaser" dog, and an emotionally detached lab assistant schooled in the use of various tubes and latex devices.) The industry has grown quickly since March 1981, when the American Kennel Club allowed registration of litters produced from frozen semen. At present, an estimated thirteen similar services across the country are helping both show-dog enthusiasts and sentimental mutt owners produce new versions of old favorites.

"We're offering people an extension on their dog's life," says Carol Bardwick, the company's founder and president. "They come in and say, 'I want a piece of him back in my life.' Dog people take this very, very seriously."

Michael Scavio, a professor of psychology at California State University, Fullerton, says the changing attitude involves more than just the willingness of America to indulge its pets. He sees in services such as Canine Cryobank and the increasingly strident animal-rights movement people who are willing to elevate animals to the level of humans a situation he says is cause for "real concern."

"I'm not sure what drives animal-rights activists so strongly that they'll commit crimes, like breaking into UCI to steal those dogs," he says, referring to a recent incident in which research animals were stolen from a laboratory at the University of California, Irvine. "Animals are not human beings, and some people fail to realize that. That's not to say there's nothing wrong with animal research. Some of their points are good. But to eliminate the research basically because of anthropomorphism, as if an animal is protected by the Constitution, is a distortion."

The increasing consumer demand for elaborate, sometimes expensive, and often gimmicky pet products may be more of a benign symptom of the same trend, but they're stacked ceiling high in ASU's sprawling warehouse, and they're among the most tangible. Tearless dog shampoos, carrot-shaped rodent wood gnaws, and stacks of books (*The Textbook of Fish Health*) are moved along a sophisticated "quick pick" order system to the packing, sealing, and labeling areas. Ordered merchandise is trundled through one of twelve loading doors onto one of ASU's seventeen delivery trucks each night.

While no single factor is driving the industry's growth, some feel that continuing changes in the traditional American family are at the heart of the trend. For individuals living alone—unmarried, widowed, divorced, empty nesters—pets represent what one psychiatrist calls an "ideal substitute child" happy to be lavished with food, clothing, and toys. And with the divorce rate hovering around 50 percent, pets often represent unconditional love and devotion to divorcing spouses and their children.

According to Scavio, pets also help their owners get in touch with a part of themselves often lost along the road from adolescence to maturity. "A lot of time, animals represent 'transitional objects' that connect us to our childhood," he says. "The animal actually is an attempt to return to that again."

The boom in pet-products sales, Scavio says, stems naturally from the fact that "you want the best for someone you love." If that sounds more like a description of a parent–child relationship, then you're beginning to grasp the scope of what experts are saying.

"To understand it, you have to break it down into three categories," says Alfred Coodley, a clinical professor emeritus of psychiatry at the University of Southern California's School of Medicine. "There are owners who have no children, wife, or husband; there are couples with no children; and there are owners who are separated or divorced and who have some custody of the children. In each case, you have a different motivation. Essentially, pets have to be clearly understood and clearly identified as children to many people. Indulging that pet with foods, with clothing, represents a further intensification of the identification of the pet as a child."

But toenail polish? "That is obviously going to be a woman who owns such a 'child,'" says Coodley. "In essence, she is training her 'daughter' to look more attractive."

Hines, of the Delta Society, says, "It's a very small percentage of the population that is super-indulgent, because there is such a thing as having a pathological attachment to one's pets. That's when a person becomes attached beyond a point that is mentally healthy to do so. But given the American system, when someone sees a need to be filled, they try to fill it. There are people who want to indulge animals and they will find a means to do it."

Dick Freeman is standing near a shelf filled with electrically heated blocks ideally suited to reptilian naps. "It's a fun industry," he says. "People that go into an auto parts store are mad because something just broke. But people that go into pet stores are there because they want to be there. The good vibes come right back to our sales people and to us."

And all this concern about anthropomorphism sounds to him like psychologists "trying to earn their money coming up with opinions." After all, the shrinks weren't there when fourteen hundred enthusiastic ASU clients toured the warehouse last November. They didn't see the smiling faces of those who walked happily away from the promotion clutching souvenir photos of themselves with a popular television personality who was on hand for the promotion.

"He was really one of the big hits of the show," Freeman says. "Spuds MacKenzie is so popular."

POSTSCRIPT

This story is adapted from one that appeared in the March 20, 1988, issue of the Orange County Register. *Since then, the arrival of big-box chain stores such as Petco and PetSmart drove a lot of small retailers out of business. Bonner sold ASU to a garden supply distributor in the Bay Area and eventually decided to start making pet products, including chew toys and rawhide bones, for sale in the big-box stores. His new company, North American Pet Products, is based in Corona, California. He says America's indulgence of its pets has not waned. It's not uncommon these days to hear owners refer to their "fur babies," for example, and a photographer in Orange County, California, who bills himself as "the Pawtographer" makes a good living posing pets in elaborate sets and dressing them in a variety of costumes, including a scuba diver, a sushi chef, or a harried business executive.*

CHAPTER TWENTY-TWO

The Life and Death of AC-3

To understand the battle to save the endangered California condor and its critical habitat, it helps to understand what happened to the last breeding female in the wild (1986)

WHEN THEY CAUGHT AC-3 FOR THE LAST TIME, IT WAS HERE, ON THE Hudson Ranch in southwestern Kern County, California. The signal from the radio transmitter under her wing indicated that the weakening California condor had been down for at least three weeks. At times she gathered enough strength to fly short distances, but she was unable to join her mate, AC-2, who returned again and again from their Santa Barbara range and soared alone overhead.

"She didn't look that bad," says Janet Hamber, the condor biologist who had tracked the pair since 1976. "She was flying some. She would flap and then sail, but she lost elevation. She did a lot of walking and resting. Eventually she just didn't have any energy." A cannon-launched net might once have been needed to capture her, but by January 3 a team from the Condor Recovery Program was able to flush AC-3 and catch her by hand.

Tests in November indicated that her blood contained trace amounts of lead, enough to worry the wildlife biologists familiar with its deadly impact on the endangered species. Still, the decision to remove one of the last known breeding female condors from her wilderness habitat was difficult, if unavoidable. When AC-3 joined twenty-one other condors

Captive-bred California condors, along with sick birds brought in for treatment, often are released back into the wild from a ridge in the Bitter Creek National Wildlife Refuge.
PHOTO BY JON MYATT, COURTESY OF THE US FISH AND WILDLIFE SERVICE, PACIFIC SOUTHWEST REGION

in captivity—four of them her own chicks—only AC-2 and four other condors remained in the wild.

She was suffering from two of the maladies that have helped drive her species to the brink of extinction. Although she had survived a hunter's blast, her head and torso were peppered with buckshot. Still, she might have lived normally if not for the lead in her belly. While feeding on a careless hunter's abandoned kill, she had ingested shotgun pellets that slowly were paralyzing her digestive system. Since 1980, at least two other lead-poisoned condors had died. She was seriously underweight, down to fourteen pounds from her normal eighteen to twenty, and despite intravenous fluids and the insertion of a feeding tube into her stomach, AC-3 starved to death at the San Diego Wild Animal Park on January 18.

The death of AC-3 was more than just the latest in a series of setbacks to the Condor Recovery Program. It ended a lifetime that included some of the most telling moments in man's effort to save the species. Understanding what happened to that particular bird during the past ten years brings into focus not only the plight of the California condor but also the plight of the scientists trying to preserve it.

The warm winds of the Hudson Ranch sweep across the southern end of the San Joaquin Valley. They rise through Bitter Creek and Santiago canyons, rippling the long grass that grows on the ridges and steep canyon walls, finally becoming the thermals that for years have drawn California condors to the skies above it.

Real estate developer Richard Hadley was drawn less by the thermals than by the potential. "When we bought the property in 1981, I don't think anyone was aware of the condor situation," says Hadley, president of Hadley Properties Inc. of Seattle. "Before we bought it, we had extensive discussions with Kern County making sure our concept was one they would like. Everybody liked the idea."

Well, not everybody. Because the condor and the developer share a fondness for this particular piece of southwestern Kern County real estate, and because the ranch in considered one of the keystones in the habitat preservation program for the disappearing condor, the US Fish and Wildlife Service is working hard to buy the ranch before Hadley has a chance to build an "agriminium" community. His latest plans call for a cluster of between 350 and 400 houses on about 4 percent of the ranch's nearly fourteen thousand acres. The developer claims the remaining 96 percent would continue as a thousand-head cattle ranch from which each resident would receive a side of beef every six months.

Wildlife biologists claim any such development would further endanger the wild condor population, which has dwindled to only a few birds, and would damage the survival chances of captive-bred condors that eventually may be released into the range. Although some people involved in the captive breeding program disagree, other condor specialists last year recommended Hudson Ranch as the best possible release site among the eight sites considered.

"The Hudson Ranch offers excellent access and visibility and is the most easily protected area for release," says Jan Riffe, chief of wildlife research for the US Fish and Wildlife Service, which along with the National Audubon Society formed the Condor Recovery Program. "It has excellent wind conditions for the newly released birds. There are few hazards such as power lines, hunting, or poisoning in the area."

Its geographic location makes the ranch central to the condors' feeding range, says John Ogden, director of ornithological research for the National Audubon Society Research Department in Tavernier, Florida. Ogden spent five years working with the condor program. "It's not just the feeding area, though," he says. "They're always passing over it, and they roost here when they're not feeding."

Condor experts have been reinforcing the species' attraction to the ranch in recent years by placing carcasses—mostly stillborn calves uncontaminated by lead or other chemicals—in visible areas of Hudson and nearby Tejon Ranch. Hudson Ranch, though, has more than easy soaring to offer the largest birds in North America. The fields are wide open, offering condors room to stretch their massive wings—a nine-foot wingspan is common—and plenty of runway room, as well as a smorgasbord view of any luckless lumps that might make a meal. The allure is such that condors have gathered here as long as anyone can remember, in flocks that once grew to a hundred birds, to gather in hunched, dark-shouldered circles.

Is it because the ranch is conveniently situated at the juncture of their wishbone-shaped range, or are they answering some call that has been ingrained in their species for millennia? "Obviously this piece of property offers something for condors," says Jesse Grantham, a staff biologist at the Condor Research Center in Ventura. "We're not sure exactly what, but why second-guess the birds?"

If that second-guess proves wrong, the knowledge will come too late, says Ron Jurek, a wildlife biologist for the California Department of Fish and Game. "Why condors have been coming back to that area is something we may never know. But you can't say, 'We'll take a look at another area that looks the same,' and consider that the same."

Beneath the mystical hyperbole lies the simple fact that the area—just a hundred miles north of downtown Los Angeles—is remarkably undeveloped. Jack Hudson, whose family homesteaded this land in the early 1890s and who shares 160 acres of the ranch with his brother, Everett, still relies on a windmill to pump his water, and fifty-six solar panels to generate his electricity. Hudson's relationship with the condors became symbiotic over the years. For instance, when his favorite cow, Elsie, died in 1984, Hudson roped her carcass to a tractor and hauled her to a hilltop near his house. She fed at least four condors, he says. The birds are "good to have around to clean up all the dead stuff."

In August 1984, the US Fish and Wildlife Service released an environmental assessment of the areas to be included in the proposed Bitter Creek National Wildlife Refuge, more than half of which is the Hudson Ranch. That report noted that while almost sixty thousand acres of condor range has been brought under federal protection since 1937, only about 1,800 acres of it is, like Hudson Ranch, foraging habitat. The service says that since Hudson is threatened with development, "we endorse any actions taken by Congress to acquire this ranch."

Negotiations for the property have been complicated by the unwillingness of both parties to compromise on a price, the alarming decline of the wild condor population, and a curious federal reassessment of the need to buy the ranch at all. Shortly after the Fish and Wildlife Service decided in December to capture all the remaining wild birds for the captive-breeding program—a decision later reversed by a federal judge—Interior Secretary Donald Hodel withdrew his support for the purchase.

"Along the line it became questionable whether the purchase was the proper thing to do," says Ben Schaefer, acting chief of the realty division at the Fish and Wildlife Service. "There aren't many condors left out in the open, and it became a question of whether it was prudent to acquire that property in view of the fact that condors may not be left in the wild."

That logic confounds the Audubon Society's John Ogden. "The decision to acquire Hudson Ranch should have in no way been related to the decision to bring the birds in. We feel it's essential to the long-term goals of the program, and it's still something of a mystery what happened in Washington."

Mark Palmer, chairman of the Sierra Club's Condor Task Force, says the federal government's willingness to back away from the Hudson Ranch purchase symbolizes its lack of commitment to its own Condor Recovery Program. "They're just trying to get out of the program as fast as their little feet can carry them," he claims, though federal officials deny the charge.

In the meantime, what may be the most critical piece of foraging habitat in the condor range remains beyond government control, and at least two condor experts—Ogden and habitat specialist Linda Blum of the Condor Research Center—suggest that the delays have had a tangible effect on the remaining wild population.

"Nobody knows where AC-3 picked up the lead that killed her, but we do know her primary place to forage was Hudson Ranch," Blum says of the female condor that died January 18. "Because the government did not get Hudson Ranch under its control, we could not control hunting there. It's entirely possible that's where she picked up the lead."

For most of her lifetime, AC-3 was about the size of a substantial Thanksgiving turkey. Although she was a marvel of aeronautical engineering, she otherwise was an aesthetic nightmare, the ultimate triumph of function over form. Her feet were gnarled, for grasping rotting flesh. Her beak was hooked, for tearing it. Her head was bald, to ease her pursuit of delectable internal organs at mealtime.

With those Pleistocene good looks, it's hard to imagine how the California condor ever captured Jan Hamber's imagination, much less that of the general public. The condor stands out on the US Fish and Wildlife Service's list of 883 endangered plant and animal species because it's the largest bird in North America and because its numbers are so few, but that doesn't fully explain why the attempt to save the condor and maintain a wild population has become one of the most ambitious and costly conservation efforts of its kind in the country.

Long before that effort got organized, Hamber was diligently tracking AC-3 and her mate for the Museum of Natural History in Santa Barbara. In 1976, two years before the Fish and Wildlife Service and the National Audubon Society joined in what has become the million-dollar-a-year Condor Recovery Program, she was doing fieldwork on "the Santa Barbara pair." The link between Hamber and the two birds was such that before becoming known as the Santa Barbara pair, and long before they were assigned the soulless scientific designations of AC-2 and AC-3—the AC meaning "adult condor" and the number indicating the order in which the wild birds were equipped with radio transmitters—the two birds were simply known as "Jan's pair."

Hamber is equal parts detached scientist and unabashed condor cheerleader, able to quote from memory ornithologist William Leon Dawson's 1923 declaration, "I am not ashamed to have fallen in love with so gentle a ghoul." On one hand, she carefully avoids unscientific conclusions about condor behavior. On the other, she let her daughter name two of AC-3's wild chicks. (While the bird's 1984 and 1985 zoo-hatched chicks bear meaningful Native American names—Malibu, Kaweah, Ojai, and Almiyi—AC-3's 1980 and 1982 wild chicks became Wilbur Pig and Bosley.)

"People go out to save all sorts of things, whether it's children, whales, or some old house," says Hamber, who now works for both the museum and the Audubon Society. "All of us are a little idealistic, and this gives some focus to life beyond our own personal survival."

She knew the birds well. She watched where they ate, roosted, and nested. She noted AC-2's peculiar habit of advertising the arrival of an egg by soaring alone above the nest for an hour or longer. She and another observer once noted AC-2's apparent courtship of another female, which they gave the vampish nickname of "Mystery Bird X," while AC-3 sat at home with an egg. On a number of occasions, she saw AC-3 behave toward a persistent, pestering offspring as any exasperated mother might. More recently, Hamber and others observed the birds coping with the loss of six eggs to the captive-breeding effort, and their reaction to the accidental deaths of two healthy chicks.

"It's difficult to watch the birds without picking up some sense of their personality, even though we're not supposed to project human characteristics," she says. "You can't help but go, 'Oh, that looks very human.'"

In 1976 and 1977, Hamber watched them hatch and fledge two chicks. Although she was unable to find their nests in 1978 and 1979, she renewed the relationship the following year after enlisting Norwalk artist John Schmitt—"one of the best field observers I know"—to help her track the pair during the winter nesting season. For weeks at a time, in the rugged San Rafael Wilderness, Schmitt waited and watched AC-2 and AC-3 as they found a cliffside ledge that suited them. It was there, in the spring of 1980, that Wilbur Pig was hatched. He was big and healthy, the more robust of the two wild condor chicks hatched that year. In its effort to monitor their progress, the newly established Condor Research Center in Ventura dispatched a team to weigh, measure, and otherwise check the health of the chicks. On June 30, while AC-2 and AC-3 were away from the nest, a two-member condor recovery team rappelled down the cliff and set about its task.

Because of his size and strength, Wilbur Pig was more difficult to handle than the other chick, which had been checked earlier. He struggled and pecked at the team member who sought him out in the corner where he retreated. He was captured and weighed, then released. He was recaptured for wing measurements, then released. He was recaptured again for beak measurement, then released. After thirty-five minutes of what ornithologists agree was unusually harsh treatment, Wilbur Pig—half of the species' entire reproductive output that year—was dead from the stress of handling.

"We were all devastated by it," Schmitt says. "It's an extremely emotional issue. There are many of us who have our own ideas about how the birds should be handled, and this immediately polarized the groups into hands-on vs. hands-off."

Hamber says the broader impact of Wilbur Pig's death was as devastating as the death itself. After the incident, the California Department of Fish and Game revoked the permit to work with the birds at a time when the Condor Recovery Program was just shifting into high gear. Plans to attach matchbook-sized radios under the wings of the remaining wild condors were set aside, and permission to carry out that critical phase of the recovery program was delayed for two years.

"That may have been the coup de grace," Hamber says of the delay. "We were within six months of making it. That probably was one of the saddest things about the program. The people who fought [for] the hands-on work were very sincere, but they helped bring on exactly what they wanted to prevent."

The division over the necessary degree of human management persists, occasionally transforming the effort to save the condor from a conservation issue into a philosophical one. When the US Fish and Wildlife Service decided to capture all the wild birds last December, for instance, the Audubon Society—the service's partner in the Condor Research Center—sued to halt the capture, and a federal judge agreed to let the birds remain free.

AC-2 and AC-3 returned to an empty nest the day Wilbur Pig died. The chick had been removed for autopsy, and although the adult birds arrived at different times, Hamber says both reacted the same way. "The first bird came in with a full crop of food for the chick," she says. "It went over to where the chick had been. It looked at the spot, then looked at the ceiling, then turned and walked along the whole shelf to a spot where the chick perched sometimes. It looked around, like it was very perplexed. Then it turned back and sat on the ledge, staring out over the canyon, then took off."

Although both birds returned to the nest several times in the days that followed, they eventually stopped coming back.

AC-3 laid two eggs in 1981. Both failed, but Hamber says there's no reason to suspect any connection between those failures and the death of Wilbur Pig the previous year. In the spring of 1982, AC-3 hatched Bosley in a small escarpment in a Santa Barbara canyon. It was one of two chicks hatched in the wild that year, and Hamber's daughter named the chick after a male character in the television show *Charlie's Angels*, and the name stuck even though the chick turned out to be a female.

If Bosley's name conjures an image of a well-meaning but clumsy nerd, the image was only reinforced by the chick's observed behavior. Although she was not yet flying at three and a half months, she was mobile enough to explore away from the nest. During one of Bosley's earliest expeditions, Hamber recalls watching her carefully work her way down to the end of the ledge, about fifty feet from the nest.

"When she got to the end, she turned around, looked back at the nest, and looked like she was wondering how to get back," she says. "She sat down and stayed there for about two hours. She finally pulled herself together and walked back up very quickly." She was nearly running as she neared the nest, Hamber says, and she practically jumped the last few feet.

By late summer of 1982, Schmitt says the chick was venturing as far as a hundred yards away from the ledge, and the observer's notes from September 13 detail one of Bosley's earliest attempts at flight. She had walked away from the ledge where AC-3 sat preening, and she was trying to make her way back toward the adult bird. In trying to get around an obstacle, Bosley took to the air. Schmitt says AC-3 watched her chick sail uncertainly past her, miss the ledge where she apparently intended to land, and disappear down and out of sight. AC-2 joined AC-3 immediately from his nearby perch, and together they walked to the edge and peered down. Bosley had parachuted about twelve feet and was sprawled in a bush. Both adult birds flew to the chick's side. They watched as she wobbled unsteadily back to the nest, and in the hour or so that followed, Schmitt says AC-3 left Bosley's side several times, walked to the edge and again peered down to where the chick had fallen.

Bosley was only a year old when she died, becoming at least the second fledgling AC-3 and her mate had lost to catastrophe. The chick was poisoned by cyanide that has been set in a "coyote-getter"—a spring-loaded trap intended to control predators—and although no one knows exactly what happened, Schmitt says he knows enough about young condors to guess. On a number of occasions, Schmitt had watched AC-2 and AC-3 pluck and "wrestle" a mountain mahogany bush on their ledge. Their chicks often did the same, he says, and that plucking might be enough to trigger such a trap. "A chick is submissive in the social hierarchy," Schmitt says. "Imagine a chick at a carcass with four or five adults. It may get pushed out and go over and start pulling at things, maybe a coyote-getter."

Bosley was the last condor chick known to have fledged in the wild. After her death and the discovery that condors could "double-clutch," the Condor Recovery Program was granted permission to take condor eggs from the nests and hatch them in zoos. "Double-clutching" is the term used to describe the process that enables a condor pair to produce a second egg during a single nesting season if the first egg is damaged or lost. Its 1982 discovery was a boost to the Condor Recovery Program, which had stalled since the death of Wilbur Pig.

By 1983, condor biologists routinely were taking eggs from the nests and spiriting them away to the participating zoos in Los Angeles and San Diego. AC-3 lost one egg to the captive breeding program that year and it hatched successfully. She lost two in the spring on 1984, only one of which was successfully hatched. The captive breeding program was showing some promise, and none too soon, because no one in the program was prepared for the winter of 1984–85.

Things had been looking up. Five of the condor pairs were breeding that year, and the biologists were working on a plan to release three captive condors back into their ten-million-acre Southern California range. "This has been a program of 'so-close,'" Hamber says. "We were so close to pulling off the plan to not only preserve the wild birds but to augment the wild population with double-clutching." During the winter, though, six of the wild birds vanished.

Investigation into the disappearances left many more questions than answers, and five are presumed dead. One of the missing birds, a male, is thought to have turned up earlier this year. It remains free, but without a radio. "To lose it all by the death of those birds was a stunning experience," Hamber says. "It was like December 7, 1941."

The winter crisis lent additional urgency to the condor program, and fortunately, AC-3 and her mate had a banner year. They produced three eggs in 1985. All were taken from their nest, and two of the three hatched successfully. The third one failed to develop.

After an egg was taken, Schmitt saw a recurring scene. In much the same way AC-2 and AC-3 seemed perplexed by the disappearance of Wilbur Pig after his death, the birds returned to their empty nest and looked around for the missing egg. They usually left and returned several times, he says, but the pair often began looking for another nesting site that same day. He says they seemed determined to breed.

If the California condor survives this foundering ark, it will be one of the lucky species. Since 1980, thirteen wild condors have died or disappeared.

Captive breeding has given the species a better chance for survival, but that small battle is being won at a time when modern science is losing a much larger war.

More than half of the 245 international conservationists, scientists, and government officials surveyed in the May–June issue of *International Wildlife* magazine said they believe that between ten thousand and one million species of plants, animals, and insects could vanish by the turn of the century. Most blame the expanding human population for the wave of extinctions.

The problems that led to the condors' decline have not disappeared. Despite efforts to preserve condor habitat, it continues to suffer the onslaught of Southern California growth; careless hunters still stalk deer and chukar—a type of partridge—across Hudson Ranch, where some condor program officials suspect AC-3 ingested the lead buckshot that eventually killed her; the Seattle-based developer who bought the Hudson Ranch in 1981 with plans to build a community there continues to haggle over the price with the US Fish and Wildlife Service, which wants to include the fourteen-thousand-acre spread in the proposed Bitter Creek Wildlife Refuge; power lines, exposed oil sumps, and coyote-getters still share the landscape with the five surviving wild birds.

From a wind-swept ridge overlooking Hudson Ranch on April 27, Chris Cogan scanned for radio signals. AC-2 had been captured five days earlier, tested for lead poisoning, and released after two days with a clean bill of health, but he hadn't been seen or heard from since. Cogan assumed the indignant condor was sulking somewhere in Santa Barbara County, but because the bird had not eaten in nine days, Cogan was beginning to worry.

He scanned AC-2's frequency at regular intervals throughout the day but found only frustrating silence. Then, in midafternoon, a signal rose high and strong out of the San Rafael Wilderness, the home range of what once had been the Santa Barbara pair. Although he couldn't see the bird, Cogan was for the moment reassured. AC-2 was out there somewhere, alone but soaring again.

POSTSCRIPT

This essay is adapted from a story that appeared in the May 18, 1986, edition of the Orange County Register. *Seven months later, with the species on the brink of extinction, wildlife biologists captured AC-3's mate, AC-2, on Bitter Creek National Wildlife Refuge, and the following year captured the last of the wild California condors remaining on Earth. Those twenty-two birds became part of a US Fish and Wildlife Service–led captive breeding program in a desperate effort to save the species. It worked. By early 2016 the condor population stood at 435 birds. Of these, 268 of them have been reintroduced into the wild, including 155 in Southern and Central California. In 2008, the program reached a milestone: for the first time since it began, more condors were flying free in the wild than were in captivity. "They've expanded their range, and they're no longer relying on human-proffered food," says Steve Kirkland, a field coordinator with the program. But the same threats persist, primarily from the ingestion of lead pellets in hunter-killed game. For example, after nineteen years in the breeding program, AC-2 was released on June 22, 2005, at the same national wildlife refuge where he was captured. Three months later, he was found dead in a remote location on the Bitter Creek refuge with elevated levels of lead in his bones, a symptom of chronic lead exposure. (Scientists can't be sure about the exact cause of death, because his carcass had been scavenged by other animals.) AC-2 left behind seventeen chicks during his life in the wild and in captivity, but Kirkland says the legacy of AC-2 and others goes far beyond that. He cites a 2012 study by researchers at the University of California, Santa Cruz, as "the smoking gun" that proved just how fatal the lead problem is for carrion-feeding wild condors. That study and others spurred the California Assembly to pass a bill in 2013 that will, by July 1, 2019, prohibit the taking of any wildlife with lead ammunition. (Hunters can instead use high-performance copper-based ammunition.) Other parts of the story have come full circle, too. AC-4, a contemporary of the pair in the story, sired thirty chicks during his three decades in captivity. And on December 22, 2015, biologists from the program climbed a ridge at the Bitter Creek refuge and released AC-4 into California's open sky, if an uncertain fate.*

CHAPTER TWENTY-THREE

SeaWorld's Six-Thousand-Pound PR Problem

What should you do when your theme park's ubiquitous and lovable mascot starts attacking people in public? (1987)

THE MOST ASTONISHING SIGHT AT SAN DIEGO'S SEAWORLD THIS PAST week had nothing to do with dancing killer whales, high-flying dolphins, or penguins roaming twelve thousand pounds of crushed ice in a "simulated Antarctic environment." It was the unexpected appearance of a gruff, intense man wearing a black fedora.

He was William Jovanovich, the fiercely private sixty-seven-year-old chairman of the board of Harcourt Brace Jovanovich, or HBJ, SeaWorld's Florida-based parent company. After steadfastly forbidding SeaWorld officials to comment on recent killer whale "accidents" and the subsequent suspension of three of the park's top executives, Jovanovich—to the surprise of the park's own public-relations staff—decided to break the corporate silence himself.

His rare public appearance underscored the acuteness of the problems that recently have plagued one of the country's most popular tourist attractions. Since a trainer had been badly injured November 21, Sea-World had said little about the increasing numbers of incidents in which the park's trademark killer whales, known generically as Shamu, had turned violent. In announcing the executive suspensions that followed,

A SeaWorld trainer communicates with one of the captive whales in San Diego, 1987.
PHOTO BY PAUL E. RODRIGUEZ, THE *ORANGE COUNTY REGISTER*. USED WITH PERMISSION.

a news release referred only to "certain measures" taken against "certain SeaWorld employees."

The problems center on SeaWorld's ubiquitous stars: the whales whose black-and-white image appears on everything from SeaWorld's letterhead to souvenir golf club covers. No one knows exactly why, but according to Jovanovich, the whales are responsible for fourteen trainer injuries since August. Some of those injuries were minor, others serious; some appeared to be accidents, others seemed to be the result of aggressive acts by the whales. Either way, the situation is comparable to the one Disneyland might face if Mickey Mouse occasionally assaulted Minnie in front of dumbfounded park visitors.

The ensuing turmoil comes less than a year after HBJ's last public crisis, which involved its controversial decision to buy—and then close—the

Marineland park in Rancho Palos Verdes in February. By relocating Marineland's two killer whales, Orky and Corky, to SeaWorld after closing the park, some whale experts say, HBJ may have sown the seeds for the injuries that followed.

The most recent, and most serious, incident involved twenty-six-year-old trainer John Sillick, who remains in fair condition at the UC San Diego Medical Center with severe damage to his ribs, pelvis, and legs. He suffered those injuries during a November 21 performance of "Shamu's Water Symphony" when Orky, one of the five whales then in SeaWorld's six-million-gallon pool, breached and landed on Sillick, who was riding on the back of another whale. A few weeks earlier, trainer Joanne Weber suffered a neck injury and another trainer was rammed in the chest during a show. It was not clear which whale or whales were involved.

The Sillick incident, film of which was broadcast on national news programs, triggered a Jovanovich-ordered internal investigation into operations at the twenty-three-year-old park. Jovanovich said a four-member investigating committee found that the suspended executives had paid little attention to the strict safety measures he had demanded only six weeks before. He also said a recent report prepared by SeaWorld's chief trainer and zoological director was "quite incomplete" in its discussion of trainer injuries.

"There was a series of accidents I had no knowledge of whatsoever," he says during his public act of contrition. "Some of the accidents were of a nature that you could argue about [the seriousness of] them, but my point of view is that human beings should never again enter the pools."

Jovanovich ordered trainers out of the whale tanks, bringing an apparent end to the most spectacular element of the three daily whale shows—the acrobatic, crowd-pleasing stunts performed by the trainers and the whales. Although he says new SeaWorld president Robert Gault disagrees with that decision, both agree that in light of recent accidents, the trainers should, for now, remain outside the tanks.

Jovanovich also says SeaWorld had let the experience level among trainers slip considerably since 1985, when chief trainer David Butcher— one of those suspended—was transferred to San Diego from SeaWorld's

Orlando, Florida, park. Jovanovich says the committee of HBJ executives he appointed to investigate the recent injuries found that "a significant number" of trainers left in 1985 because they disagreed with Butcher's training method, which requires whales to trust and obey trainers without predictable food rewards and which hinges on the quality of the relationship between humans and the giant mammals. "Put crudely, it's intimacy versus feeding," Jovanovich says.

Whale experts outside SeaWorld say the reward system itself is not to blame, but rather the fault lies in SeaWorld's inability to keep trainers long enough for the whales to establish trusting relationships. Admitting "negligence" and "serious mistakes" on the part of his subordinates, Jovanovich subsequently suspended Butcher, SeaWorld president Jan Schultz, zoological director Lanny Cornall, and public relations director Jackie Hill, although Hill eventually was reinstated. Severance discussions are expected to begin with the other three this week, Jovanovich says.

In addition, he announced a number of changes in Shamu Stadium, the new $12.5-million-dollar, 3,500-seat arena where the whales perform, including installation of a $3-million-dollar video screen with underwater cameras. Says Tim Desmond, a whale trainer and former assistant curator of Marineland: "My opinion from a distance is that SeaWorld has initiated some major changes that are very positive."

The changes, however, come long after word began spreading about problems at SeaWorld. "Since last January I've been hearing about the killer whale accidents," says Dennis Kelly, an Orange Coast College marine biology professor and killer whale specialist. "This last accident was just the icing on the cake."

If true, the problems began about the same time HBJ bought Marineland. Two months after purchasing the marine park in December 1986, HBJ closed it in what opponents charge was an elaborate effort to acquire its two killer whales. Orky was one of the few male whales in SeaWorld's collection of twelve whales, and as such he is critical to SeaWorld's breeding program. That program, which has produced only one surviving baby whale, is increasingly important because public outcry prevented SeaWorld from capturing wild killer whales off the West Coast and Alaska during 1983 and 1984. The breeding program also is critical because HBJ is preparing to open its fourth SeaWorld park in San Antonio, Texas, next year.

Opponents say SeaWorld mishandled the transfer of Orky and Corky from Rancho Palos Verdes to San Diego, and that that may help explain some of the recent incidents. Killer whales are among some of the sea's most intelligent creatures, and they have elaborate social units commonly called pods. Not only had Orky and Corky shared the same pool since 1969, bonding into a two-member pod, but they also had worked with the same trainers for much of that time.

After HBJ closed Marineland, the two whales were moved into an unfamiliar SeaWorld pool already occupied by the park's three female whales. Orky and Corky's longtime trainers say SeaWorld trainers weren't particularly interested in their advice on how to handle the former Marineland residents. Since then, two more female whales—brought to San Diego for the winter from SeaWorld's Ohio park—have been placed in the same pool.

Kelly says the potential for trouble should have been obvious. In addition to being unfamiliar with one another, he says, the whales are of different ages and maturity levels. They're accustomed to different training techniques, are working with less experienced trainers, and were captured in vastly different regions of the world. "It's as difficult to resolve as putting an American into a room full of Russians," says Kelly.

Further complicating the integration of Orky and Corky into the new environment was Orky's unpredictability. Former Marineland curator Desmond says Orky deliberately dunked him in November 1977 and nearly killed another trainer six months later by pinning her to the bottom of the pool. Desmond says he suspects the incidents were tied to the fact that Corky was pregnant at the time, but as a result Orky had not had a trainer in the water with him since 1978.

"I think SeaWorld tried to do too much too soon," says Kelly. "The orcas weren't mad at anybody. There was just so much going on. Unfortunately, all those people ended up in the hospital."

For a corporation whose fortunes are so closely tied to the killer whale, the recent events have been a nightmare. The 135-acre SeaWorld park on San Diego's Mission Bay drew more than three million visitors last year, making it sixth in attendance among the top ten US theme parks. Although Jovanovich claims "killer whales are not the whole of Sea-World, for God's sake," they certainly are its most visible component.

From the moment adult visitors pay their $17.95 at SeaWorld ticket booths, which bear the familiar killer whale logo, they are inundated by Shamu's black-and-white image. They can sip a cool drink at the Shamu Frosted Lemonade Stand. Their children, whose admission costs $11.95, can ride in black-and-white killer whale–shaped strollers. Given that level of corporate commitment, some feel Jovanovich's uncharacteristic appearance this week isn't so hard to understand.

"He's been characterized as a strong, bottom-line sort of guy," says Bryant Winchell of Palos Verdes Estates, founder of a citizens group that vigorously fought SeaWorld's closure of Marineland. "He's got a brand new, very expensive SeaWorld opening up in San Antonio. It seems like he's gonna need more orcas, and they've already been burned in Alaska and Washington [state]. All of a sudden, here's this man saying, 'Aw shucks, gee whiz. We've had some problems and this is what I did to correct it.' There's got to be a reason for that, and I don't believe it's senility."

Winchell says he thinks Jovanovich is taking "strategic action" that might make it easier for SeaWorld to muffle public concern if it someday wants to capture more whales. However, Jim Lecky of the National Marine Fisheries Service, says SeaWorld hasn't applied for a permit to capture more whales. "It's sort of an irony," Lecky says. "SeaWorld has done a lot in those parks to stimulate interest in the killer whales that have now become an impediment. The level of awareness of the public and the concern for individual animals now stands in the way of their receiving a permit."

That irony is of no concern to Winchell, who continues to wonder about the unusual visit from the man in the fedora. "The fact that he came out and stood in front of those lights and cameras is very significant. There's something he wants. The battle isn't over yet."

POSTSCRIPT

*This essay is adapted from a story that appeared in the December 13, 1987,
edition of the* Orange County Register. *Since then, HBJ, primarily a book
publisher, sold its theme parks to Anheuser-Busch Co., best known for making
beer. SeaWorld eventually allowed trainers back into the whale pools. In 2009,
Busch Entertainment was sold to the Blackstone group, a New York City–
based multinational private-equity investment banking, asset management,
and financial services firm. Blackstone, in turn, sold much of SeaWorld Entertainment in an initial public offering in 2013—the same year documentary
film director Gabriela Cowperthwaite's* Blackfish *premiered at the Sundance
Film Festival. That film, a searing indictment of SeaWorld's killer whale program and the cruelties of whale captivity, focused on Tilikum, an orca involved
in the deaths of three people, including trainer Dawn Brancheau. The film has
been widely shown on television by CNN Films, and SeaWorld's very large
public relations problem continues. SeaWorld Parks & Entertainment now
has twenty-three orcas in its US theme parks, where attendance has dropped
steadily since 2013 despite aggressive discounts on ticket prices. By early 2016,
SeaWorld San Diego had abandoned a hundred-million-dollar plan to expand
its killer whale tanks and decided to use some of the money to instead build a
submarine ride. Shortly after that, CEO Joel Manby announced plans to end
SeaWorld's orca breeding program and phase out its theatrical killer whale
shows; by then, the star of SeaWorld's television commercials was a beluga
whale named Martha.*

CHAPTER TWENTY-FOUR

Aren't We All Just Squatters, Really?

Grappling with the karmic implications of a house I don't deserve (2004)

THE CABLE INSTALLATION GUY WAS THE FIRST TO SEE ME SQUIRM. HE was standing slack-jawed in the front entryway of the forty-five-hundred-square-foot bluff-top home into which we'd just moved. He stared across the expansive dining room and through the floor-to-ceiling glass doors at a sweeping wide-angle view of Santa Monica Bay framed by dramatic cliffs that tumble to the sea.

"Whoa," he said.

"See, here's the thing," I explained, "we don't own it. We're not rich. We're just caretakers. Squatters, really."

He looked at his paperwork. My name. This address. "But you live here?"

"It's not what you think."

Like he cared. "Whoa."

How this happened is a complicated story involving my wife's job. Trust me, it probably won't happen to you. By any measure of fairness, it never should have happened to a family of middle-class Midwest transplants whose previous idea of living large meant expanding an 813-square-foot California bungalow to 1,100 square feet. But it did happen, and for the past few years my family has been fortunate enough to live in a borrowed house situated on one of the most breathtaking and unavailable pieces of property in Southern California. How did I get here?

I have no answer. Dumb luck? Great timing? Hard work? Coincidence? All those things. Regardless, we are raising our children in this house. For much of that time I've felt like a valet-parking attendant in a Lamborghini, a transient in thrift-store Armani, the Little Leaguer on the Yankees bench. People see where I live and assume I'm a man of wealth, success, and social status. But in my mind I'm living the life of an Enron executive—extravagant, inappropriate, and wholly unearned. Which is why I'm compelled to puncture the illusion for visitors, to convince the cable guy that I'm not who I appear to be.

Friends tell me to relax and enjoy living above my means, but a home is so much more than a shelter, a status symbol, or a place to put

This roosting owl was the patriarch of a family that for years hunted along the cliffs surrounding the author's home in Palos Verdes Estates, California.
PHOTO BY MARTIN J. SMITH

your stuff. It's a statement about who you are, or who you perceive yourself to be. When you're living in someone else's house—someone very different from who you are—it's like trying on their skin. If it doesn't fit, there are issues. Foremost among them, I struggle with the fear that this stroke of good fortune has put me in a whopping karmic hole. Reincarnation promises nothing for me but leprosy, lice, and savagery. If my debt comes due in this life, I could find myself playing center for the Clippers, or being Martha Stewart's cellmate, or a contestant on *The Apprentice*.

I cope by trying to explain. "It's a long story, and it has nothing to do with talent, success, or money," I now tell astonished first-time visitors. "Feel free to resent me anyway."

Thing is, this place that doesn't fit and isn't mine has changed me in ways both powerful and unexpected. In gratitude for our good fortune, I plunged into community service. Four years as the local Cubmaster. Three years as a commissioner for the local soccer league. I pitch batting practice, line sports fields, repair goal nets, pick up after litterbugs. The community where I once felt like an intruder gradually became our home. Still, those efforts were not enough, because although some people can afford to live in so lovely a place, no one less than Mother Teresa truly deserves it.

Eventually, I looked inward for answers. Before this house, I was an agnostic. Now, every morning when I let the dog out, I stand humbly in a backyard at the very edge of the continent and pray my gratitude, because for a blessing like this surely there must be someone to thank.

Lately, I've sensed another change. Something inside me wants to possess this place, to make it mine. I know this because I've had a recurring, telltale dream. In it, years from now, I'm on a boat and looking up at the cliff upon which this house is perched. I am trying, earnestly and futilely, to convince a fellow tourist along the port rail that, yes, I really did once live in that house up there on the hill. It was never really mine, I'm careful to explain, but for a period of my life I ate my morning cereal in its kitchen and sipped sugared coffee on its decks. I could lie in a hammock with our kids and watch red-tailed hawks and owls hunt the nearby canyons. With binoculars, I watched spouting whales through the window by the stove, and from that same spot once tracked a pod of dolphins for an hour.

And there, at the far end of the lot, is a pet cemetery that holds the ashes or remains of our family menagerie, including dogs Belle and Vinnie, Mom the fancy rat, Speedy the bearded dragon, dwarf hamsters Buddy and Dale, and a goldfish named Sushi. On summer nights, through our open bedroom doors, we could hear the crashing surf and the sharp bark of seals. About once a week, at dusk, a bagpiper trekked down the winding dirt path to the middle of the cove below, and we would eat dinner to the rising, mournful sound of "Amazing Grace."

"*Riiight*," the tourist says just before sidling away to find a new spot on the starboard side.

In some ways I hate that dream. It reminds me that this house—this place of both powerful discomfort and unexpected joy in my life—is not mine, that it never was and never will be. It reminds me that we will have to leave it someday and find another place to live. I vowed from the beginning to always keep that in mind, to never forget that we're just passing through, squatters in paradise.

On the other hand, I love that dream. It reminds me that, in a broader sense and regardless of what we own, we're all just passing through, squatters in paradise. It reminds me, too, that where I've lived has become part of who I am, and that's something I'll have forever.

POSTSCRIPT

This essay is adapted from one that originally appeared in the October 24, 2004, issue of the Los Angeles Times. *Thanks to the generosity of the City of Palos Verdes Estates, California, where my wife was a manager, our family lived in this city-owned home overlooking Santa Monica Bay for nearly fifteen years, raising our kids there. When my wife retired in 2013, we moved out. Two years later, the house, along with several adjacent city-owned homes, was dismantled and the lots graded into open space. The good news: Our pet cemetery appears to have been undisturbed by the demolition and lot grading.*

Acknowledgments

I FIRST BEGAN ASSEMBLING THIS COLLECTION OF ESSAYS AND STORIES IN 2015 as a gift for our children, Lanie and Parker, who grew up in Southern California but really had no idea how our family ended up here or what first attracted their father to the place in the mid 1980s. I wanted them to know *my* story.

At that point, I'd been a journalist in Pennsylvania for more than six years, during a period of bone-rattling economic and social change. The American steel industry was melting down. Like a lot of people in western Pennsylvania, my father, who worked for US Steel for forty-two years, was sucked into the downward spiral. Its effects on me weren't just personal, but professional. As a newspaper reporter for the now-defunct *Pittsburgh Press*, I wrote a lot of stories about that decline and the social fallout from it, including financial devastation, home foreclosures, domestic and workplace violence, all of it.

Then I got an offer to work for a newspaper in Southern California, the *Orange County Register*, where at the time the stories had a decidedly different flavor. Many of them were about growth, affluence, and people taking bold risks. The housing market was booming, and the population was growing. Two well-financed local newspapers, the *Register* and the *Los Angeles Times*, were fighting a turf war for educated and affluent readers. Kids were driving Ferraris to their senior proms. The papers were publishing stories about whales—*whales!*—on the front page. In short, Southern California was the opposite of where I grew up, and I was drawn, like so many other refugees, to that warm and sunny place. I arrived as an eager eyewitness.

My life as a writer in the West has been one of endless fascination and opportunity. I was helped along that road by many people to whom I owe a great debt. My early training came from journalism professors at the Pennsylvania State University such as R. Thomas Berner and the late Eugene Goodwin, and colleagues such as my longtime friend and occasional collaborator, Patrick J. Kiger. I dedicate this book to them. The *Register*'s metro editor, Robert Ostmann Jr., offered me a reporting job that, for a while at least, allowed me to range far and wide throughout the western United States. Both he and features editor Richard Cheverton encouraged my often outlandish story ideas and trusted that I could pull them off, while the paper underwrote my travel and other costs as I reported them. It was a different era of newspaper journalism, and I was its happy beneficiary.

I changed employers a few times, but everywhere I went I had the same support from extraordinary editors, including Alice Short, Drex Heikes, Bob Sipchen, and Pamm Higgins at the *Los Angeles Times Magazine*. At *Orange Coast* magazine, former publisher Ruth Ko and later the extraordinary editorial team at the magazine and its corporate parent, Emmis Communications, became my journalistic enablers. I thank them all.

Essayist and former *Los Angeles Times* book editor David L. Ulin was kind enough to write the book's thoughtful foreword. Sherry Monahan, president of the Western Writers of America, listened to my idea for this collection and promptly put me in touch with editor Erin Turner of Globe Pequot, who thankfully recognized in it the same potential that I did. I'm grateful to them both for letting me share what has been a sustained and extraordinary three-decade joyride through the American Southwest.

—Martin J. Smith

About the Author

Martin J. Smith is a journalist, magazine editor, and winner of more than fifty newspaper and magazine writing awards. A former senior editor of the *Los Angeles Times Magazine* and former editor-in-chief of *Orange Coast*, the magazine of Orange County, California, he's the author of five critically acclaimed suspense thrillers, including *Time Release, Shadow Image, The Disappeared Girl, Straw Men*, a 2002 Edgar Award nominee, and the more recent *Combustion*. He also has authored or coauthored three nonfiction books, including *The Wild Duck Chase*, upon which the award-winning 2016 documentary film *The Million Dollar Duck* is based, and with Patrick J. Kiger wrote two nonfiction books of pop-culture history, including *Poplorica: A Popular History of the Fads, Mavericks, Inventions, and Lore That Shaped Modern America*, and *OOPS: 20 Life Lessons From the Fiascoes That Shaped America*. After more than three decades as a journalist based in Southern California, he currently lives and writes in Granby, Colorado.